WHITEFELLA JUMP UP

Germaine Greer is a renowned writer, academic and broadcaster. Her books include *The Female Eunuch*, *The Change*, *The Whole Woman* and *The Boy*. She is Professor of English and Comparative Studies at the University of Warwick. Born in Melbourne and educated in Australia and at Cambridge University, she currently divides her time between England and her rainforest property on the Queensland–NSW border.

GERMAINE GREER

WHITEFELLA JUMP UP

The Shortest Way to Nationhood

P
PROFILE BOOKS

First published in Great Britain in 2004 by
Profile Books Ltd
58A Hatton Garden
London EC1N 8LX
www.profilebooks.co.uk

First printed in Australia in 2003 by *Quarterly Essay*

10 9 8 7 6 5 4 3 2

Typeset in Minion by MacGuru
info@macguru.org.uk

Printed and bound in Great Britain by
Bookmarque Ltd, Croydon, Surrey

A CIP catalogue record for this book is available from the British Library.

ISBN 1 86197 739 5

CONTENTS

jump up, from Kriol, of cattle, to leap up to a higher level; hence, of people, to be resurrected or reborn.

I

THE WHITE MAN'S BURDEN

What follows is not another of the hundreds of studies of Aborigines that are published every year. Neither is it the nth paper bullet shot off in support of the black arm-banded or the white blind-folded. Its author has not studied a particular remnant of the original populations of this country as if they were stone-age pond-life, nor has she read more than a few hundred thousands of the billions of words written about Aborigines by ethnographers, ethnologists, ethologists, psychologists, anthropologists, archaeologists, sociologists, linguists, semiologists, historians, glottochronologists and graduate students. All such are welcome to make what they will of a modest suggestion offered by an elderly Australian laywoman who is not in search of a qualification or a job or promotion. I would hope that what I have to say will be recognised as grounded in simple commonsense, but I confidently expect that among the comments that will be made, if any are made, will be that I have lost my marbles, to which others, whom the media recognise as my friends, will obligingly rejoin that "Germs" was always crazy and this no more than the latest manifestation of her ratbaggery. Above all I'm not trying to be right at the cost of proving everyone else wrong. I'm offering a suggestion for consideration, discussion and modification, in the hope of bouncing a tired and rancorous discourse onto new tracks. Where it goes after that is not up to me.

There is only one way to escape from an impasse, that is, to turn back to the point where you went wrong, sit down on the ground and have a think about it.

I've seen too much of the frantic grief that is eating the heart out of Aboriginal communities not to have racked my brain for years trying to imagine a way of healing it, but I'm not here offering yet another solution to the Aborigine problem. Rather I want to suggest an end to the problematisation of Aborigines. Blackfellas are not and never were the problem. They were the solution, if only whitefellas had been able to see it. The country I love has been crazily devastated by whitefellas who seem unable to give a damn, and who even now insist on continuing in their madness, knocking down its mountains, grinding up its trees, diverting its watercourses, building high-rises on its flood plains, creating an endless nightmare of suburbia from which our kids try to escape by sticking needles in their arms. I want to turn the situation upside down and see if it wouldn't run better that way.

My white countrymen appear to me afflicted by a kind of emotional paralysis, a pathological indifference. It is obvious to anyone who gives the matter five minutes' thought that Australia's "sophisticated recreational lifestyle" comes at a huge cost in terms of non-renewable resources, water for instance. The senescent bush along the densely populated foreshores will one day explode in firestorms that will wipe out the insurance market and bring the whole shonky economy to its knees. Australians have access to adequate and reliable information about the threat represented by their mismanaged environment, but they remain unable to give a damn.

A good deal of energy has been expended on diagnosing the malaise that leads to high levels of alcoholism, addiction and crimes of violence in Aboriginal society; there are as many explanations of Aboriginal self-destructiveness as there are writers on the subject.

Whitefella spiritual desolation is seldom admitted, let alone discussed. Problem drinking affected whitefellas long before it made devastating inroads into Aboriginal society, and it continues to wreak havoc today. Drinking habits that are well known to be implicated in violence of all kinds, especially domestic violence and child abuse, as well as road accidents, avoidable illness, suicide and premature death, are regarded with a kind of amused tolerance. When we see such behaviour in Russia we know it to be pathological and we can diagnose demoralisation, displacement and despair as root causes, without invoking cop-out theories of alcoholism as a disease caused by genetically inherited factors.

Early observers of Australian drunkenness posited a disease they called dipsomania; others treated alcohol itself as a race poison. The powers of the demon drink were wildly exaggerated, as by Charles Eden, writing in *My Wife and I in Queensland. An Eight Years Experience in the above colony*, published in 1872:

> Once taste the degrading debauch, and there is no remedy, the victim goes on knocking down his cheque half-yearly, sinking lower and lower, all that was ever good in him withering and drying up under the curse,

> and he dies alone at last unknown, unregretted and unmissed. This may seem a terrible picture but, reader, it is underdrawn.

If whitefellas are wrecking their lives and the lives of others because of the way they abuse alcohol, it is not because alcohol is itself addictive, but because something has gone badly wrong. That something has been wrong from the beginning of settlement and it has yet to be put right.

It seems obvious that convicts and settlers bartered with the military for a share of their rum ration during the first years of settlement because they were seeking an anodyne to their shock, disorientation and misery. They were in the wrong place and they knew it. It was clear to the captains of ships trading with the colony that they had an inexhaustible market for vast quantities of rum. In 1794 the captain of an American ship refused to supply provisions to the starving colony unless the governor also relieved him of his cargo of 7500 gallons of rum. Rum became currency; wages were paid in rum. In 1797 Governor Hunter was appalled to find "spirits enough to deluge the colony" being sold to the settlers "at an immense profit, to the destruction of all order, to the almost total destruction of every speck of religion". Between 1800 and 1802 when D'Arcy Wentworth and his mates held an exclusive licence for the importation of liquor, 69,980 gallons of spirits and 33,246 gallons of wine were landed in Sydney, to be consumed by a population of less than 6000. John MacArthur, much-lauded founder of the Australian pastoral industry, was only the first landowner to solve his cash crisis by dealing in alcohol. Many others followed his example. The first thing John Pascoe Fawkner did after choosing the site for the future city of Melbourne was to build, not a church or a town hall, but a hotel. It was accepted that without alcohol life in the Great South Land would be unbearable.

For convicts and settlers of Irish background, it was second nature to set aside part of any crop of grain or potatoes for distilling poteen. With spirits retailing at high prices, and the land refusing to produce the hoped-for riches, many of the settlers turned to sly-grog manufacture as a way of making ends meet. Even the most remote rural tracks were studded with shanties or sly-grog shops, run on the lines of the shebeens in Ireland. What was sold in them was a dangerous mixture of ethyl and methyl alcohols, which could drive a man off his head, or leave him blind, or dead. Not for nothing did Banjo Paterson call the shanty where sheep-stealer Ryan was found "drunk as a lord" by Trooper Scott the "Shadow of Death Hotel". Inland Australian townships were little more than strings of pubs, where the publicans and their employees were expert at "lambing down", filling the pastoral worker with grog in order to separate him from his pay-cheque. Drunks were left to sleep it off where they fell, sometimes in the filth of the gutter, where the sun completed the dehydration that the liquor had begun. Ruinous drinking habits did not change as the colony grew; wherever the settlers went alcohol followed, and workers in every branch of the pastoral industry if they got their hands on alcohol would drink it to the last drop, unless it killed them first.

Drinking is now so deeply embedded in Australian culture that it is perceived as normal, healthy even. In *Gone Bush* Bob Lunney spins a yarn about life in Darwin at the beginning of the fifties: a rugby-playing mate of his was suffering from kidney cramps and went to see the doctor:

> The doctor was a bit mystified, and then … he asked timidly, as if he thought it was a stupid question, "You do drink beer, don't you?" [He didn't.] "Bloody hell!" ex-

> plained the doctor, "no wonder you've got kidney cramps, you silly bugger. You're the first patient I've had up here over sixteen, male or female, who doesn't drink. Drink two beers a day to flush your kidneys or pack your traps and go back south."

This advice is both apocryphal and bad, but it illustrates the universality of the belief that alcohol consumption is an essential marker of the good life, and tangentially, of adulthood. Lunney goes on:

> He drank his two beers a day and the cramps disappeared, but unfortunately when last I saw him he was an alcoholic bum.

In prissy white-collar twenty-first-century Australia, a culture of macho hard-drinking still prevails. As Frank Moorhouse says in his essay "The Australian Legend" (1984), "Heroic spree-drinking still characterises males of many sub-classes [*sic*]. Drinking is a man's way of crying, as Lawson said." For Moorhouse and Lawson before him it seems obvious that self-punishing bouts of drinking have a strong connection with grief of some kind. For whatever reason it remains easier in most places in Australia to get drunk than to find something half-way decent to eat. In towns like Alice Springs, liquor outlets outnumber food stores by a ratio of six or seven to one. One in three Australian men will exhibit symptoms of alcoholism at some time in his life; 15 per cent of Australian alcoholics will kill themselves by violent means; more will just drink themselves to death. Binge drinking is one of a galaxy of self-destructive behaviours making a continuum with suicide, suicide attempts, drug abuse, reckless driving and self-harming, all of which are rife in the "lucky" country.

What is there for whitefellas to cry about? Explanations of Australian binge-drinking are lame, but they do contain some clues. Henry Lawson's Joe Wilson explains it this way:

> Shepherds and boundary riders, who are alone for months, must have their periodical spree at the nearest shanty, else they'd go raving mad. Drink is the only break in the awful monotony, and the yearly or half-yearly spree is the only thing they've got to look forward to: it keeps their minds fixed on something definite ahead.

Country is only awfully monotonous to those who are uninterested in it and unattached to it. Lawson and his characters Mitchell and Joe Wilson are typical in their downright loathing of the outback, "a blasted barren wilderness that doesn't even howl". The wilderness was not in fact barren, and at least until whitefellas fenced off vast areas to serve as test sites and rocket ranges it was not blasted either.

In Australian literature, the Europeans' corrosive unease expresses itself in a curious distortion of the pathetic fallacy, which characterises the land as harsh, cruel, savage, relentless, the sky as implacable, pitiless and so forth. The heart of the country is called "dead". As Thomas Keneally said in "On Being Australian" (1984), if we call the heart of our nation dead we render ourselves "reduced humans, cultural and geographic maggots". But it is not the heart of the country but the gubba's heart that is dead, empty of attachment, and petulant under the penalty of Adam. In our literature vicissitudes of heat and cold are interpreted as a kind of punishment and the physical world itself given the role of an avenging deity. The vegetation is described as "stunted", "warped", "misshapen", "gnarled and twisted and ragged", another example of projection of a presentiment of evil within to the countryside without. Michael Blakemore in "The Straight Poofter", published in 1984, describes the landscape as "endless and neutral, not hostile to human beings, nor nurturing; just profoundly indifferent", and again we are contemplating another transference; it is Blakemore who is indifferent to country, here revealingly called "landscape". It was not the country that was damned but the settler who felt in his heart that he was damned. His impotent cursing, which has left a legacy in the unequalled degree of profanity in Australian speech, was a classic piece of transference. We hate this country because we cannot allow ourselves to love it. We know in our hearts' core that it is not ours.

Migration, especially to a land from which there can be no return, is invariably traumatic, but the stress that followed was exacerbated for Australian settlers to become the kind of unremitting and inadmissible psychic pain that demands escape into oblivion, for which the culture of drunken jollity provided an acceptable mask. It is my belief that the pain that the alcohol was meant to kill was complicated by deeply repressed shame and guilt. The settlers did not mean to destroy the Aborigines, but they could not deny that the Aborigines were being destroyed. They could agree not to mention the fact but they could not forget it. Their descendants prefer to bicker over just how badly whitefellas treated blackfellas and just how much or how little the blackfellas deserved it, rather than utter the simple word "sorry". John

Howard's stubbornness on the issue was certainly politically expedient, but it also demonstrated once more the whitefella's inability to come to terms with his own history in Australia. Saying sorry would not have fixed anything, but it might have reaped the whirlwind, as Australians came to wonder just what it was that they were saying sorry for. Admitting that one is sorry is tantamount to confessing that one is sad, and Australians are supposed to be happy-go-lucky. Australians can aver "She'll be right, mate!" in the teeth of disaster.

Such self-destructive denial is part and parcel of the pathology of colonialism. Four hundred years of humiliation and unrevenged outrage at the hands of the English may explain why it is that the Irish still consume more alcohol per head than any other nation in the world. This pathology they imported with them to Australia, where they found themselves once more under the control of Anglo authorities. Whether they were directly involved in the atrocities committed against Aboriginal people or not, they must have been aware that black Australians were suffering the same agonies as the "black Irish" in the old country, when their religion was ridiculed as barbarous heresy, their lands taken up by foreigners and they and their families reviled and humiliated as depraved savages. Some such unrecognised remorse could be what drove the Celtic part of the Anglo-Celt majority into crazy postures of denial, so that they insisted on discovering a country that was already well known, and fantasised about gaining total control over vast tracts in which they couldn't have survived without the assistance of those whose claim they tacitly denied, and indulged visions of wealth in plain defiance of the ruling regimes of drought and flood, only to drop everything and dash back and forth across the country in desperate pursuit of any rumour of a gold strike. The British elite may have caught the madness from the Irish; those who eventually came out on top were the ones who held aloof, bided their time, bought up the ruined and rented their selections back to them, acquired mining rights and sheep runs and cattle leases by the dozen, and had the capital to exploit all of them. The winners were no saner than the battlers; their delusion was their utter conviction of their own mental and moral superiority and their God-given right to civilise and subjugate all other groups in the Great South Land.

The settlers toiled like madmen to remove the scrub, bush and trees that stood in the way of cultivation. They no more realised that the newly denuded land would be vulnerable to extremes of heat and cold, drought and flood than they realised that the rising of the watertable would bring the stored salts to the surface, gradually poisoning the land cleared with so much blood, sweat and tears. Nor did they realise that the willows they planted along the waterways, the trees so beloved of writers like Lawson and Paterson, would spread through entire river systems, until the flows were clogged, or that their garden flowers would become a curse. The settlers imagined that they were redeeming a land that the original inhabitants had failed to manage in any rational fashion, and that they could turn it into a new Canaan. What gave them the right to displace the original inhabitants – they thought – was their fealty to the biblical command to earn their bread by the sweat of their brows, in which duty – they thought – hunter-gatherers were derelict and so forfeited any right of ownership they might be said to possess. The argument was pure sophistry, because it depended on identifying tilling and herding as the only activities that could be called work; in any case the newcomers had only the vaguest idea of how Aborigines got a living off the land. They did not suspect, until it was too late, that the "virgin" territory they were claiming for themselves was actually a man-made resource. The only thing that could ease the settlers' deepest suspicions about the rightness of their enterprise would have been success, which would prove that God had blessed it. Instead failure followed failure.

The settlers' desperate longing to recreate their homelands is easy to understand and sympathise with, but homesickness is not the whole story. The imaginary patchwork of neat farms punctuated by pretty villages with churches and tidy towns with law courts and concert halls attended by happy small farmers and their jolly families had never existed in the old country. The very concept derived from a view of "Merrie England" that was no more real than Tolkien's bucolic Middle Earth. For some such dream the settlers fought the bush to a standstill and lost. Lawson's early story "Settling on the Land" (published in 1896) tells how Tom Hopkins struggled to grub out trees on land he was not even sure of owning, and eventually managed to clear a patch.

> Tom ploughed and sowed wheat, but nothing came up to speak of – the ground was too poor; so he carted stable manure six miles from the nearest town, manured the land, sowed another crop and prayed for rain. It came. It raised a flood which washed the crop clean off the selection, together with several acres of manure, and a considerable

> portion of the original surface soil; and the water brought down enough sand to make a beach, and spread it over the field to a depth of six inches.

Lawson and his readers seem perfectly to understand that the farmers' Herculean struggle was misconceived and misdirected, and that instead of creating a new land they were destroying an old one. The disaster of the closing of the mouth of the Murray is prefigured in this story written when the colony had been in existence barely a century, nowadays a human lifespan. Tom tries dairying, with dire consequences for both the unfortunate beasts and Tom, tries sheep and is worsted by the squatter. Long since he had begun to curse Australia.

> Tom was admitted to the lunatic asylum at Parramatta next year, and the squatter was sent there the following summer, having been ruined by the drought, the rabbits, the banks and a wool-ring.

Lawson tells Tom Hopkins's story in as few words as possible, with a dry deadpan humour that suggests, better than hair-tearing could do, the irrationality of the whole project. Tom's one regret was "that he wasn't found to be of unsound mind before he went up-country". Paterson's cattleman Kiley fared no better

But droughts and losses came apace
    To Kiley's Run
Till ruin stared him in the face;
He toiled and toiled while lived the light,
He dreamed of overdrafts at night:
At length because he could not pay
His bankers took the stock away
    From Kiley's Run.

When Kiley died of a broken heart his run was taken over and renamed Chandos Park Estate by an absentee landlord living in England. The once-bustling homesteads and out-buildings stood empty, but for "a half-paid overseer".

Ultimately rural Australia ended up emptier than it was before it was "opened up". Australia has now the most highly urbanised population of any country in the world. The process was already advanced when Lawson and Steele Rudd began writing about rural Australia in the 1890s for an urban and suburban readership. The whitefellas who tried to make a living in the bush soon fled from it, and wound up as far from the interior as they could get, on the continent's very edge where they built themselves houses that faced outwards and away, across the ocean. Happiness is now a house in a seaside suburb with not a single native plant in sight. Most Australians would these days deny that they hate the land, but actions speak louder than words. Try going into a main street bookstore and asking for books on Australian natural history, and you'll see what I mean. You will be offered a book on gardening (with exotics) or breeding cats or fishing. Substantial books on Australian flora and fauna, ecology and geology are occasionally published, but they aren't sold. As Judith Wright said in her essay "Australia – Landscape Ancient and Modern" (1984), "our revulsion from the country is still with us, and is one of the reasons for our continued ill-treatment of it". The NSW Rural Fire Service chief, Phil Koperberg, remarked to Ashley Hay after the last ruinous bout of wildfire in the Blue Mountains, "It's a weird country. You wonder what the hell we're doing here."

To a jaundiced eye the much-vaunted hedonistic Australian lifestyle appears shot through with a kind of raucous hysteria, exemplified in phenomena like the greatest outback knees-up of them all, the phantasmagoric Birdsville Races. Thousands of people in thousands of vehicles make for what used to be a hub of Aboriginal transcontinental travelling, as fast as they can go, so they can fetch up at preordained campsites and wateringholes where they can indulge in alcohol-fuelled bonhomie with strangers. Once in Birdsville they assemble at the race-track at midday for a few hours' drinking and betting, before spending the evenings just drinking, until the road-ways are submerged by a tide of cans and the pile of bottles behind the Birdsville Hotel is bigger than the building. Then they all depart, leaving Birdsville to the cattle-trucks and the hundred or so people who live there all year round. Some will take the inner road and pit their four-wheel drives against Big Red, the biggest sandhill in Australia, in yet one more example of the endless game of whitefella versus country. The annual trek to the Birdsville Races is a pilgrimage to nowhere. Similar paradigms of displacement activity such as Henley-on-Todd and the Mindil Beach beer-can regatta pop up wherever there is a hook to hang them on. Common to them all is an element of mockery of self and of country. Anybody who finds such frantic and motiveless jollification disturbing will be told to lighten up, not to take things so seriously. And so the culture of denial perpetuates itself.

Australian culture used to be anti-bullshit; Australians

now lend themselves to every kind of threadbare cultism, instant religion and DIY spirituality, all focused on the individual, all promising the inner peace that whitefellas know they don't deserve. A ragbag culture of self-improvement has concentrated the individual's focus more and more upon himself, his self-esteem, his energy levels, his purity, whatever. Not a surviving fragment of rainforest but is not infested with people communing with themselves and submitting to the guidance of shamans and charlatans of every kidney, expert at solving everyone's problems but their own.

As all his dreams crashed around him and all his hard work came to nought, the settler of literature was sometimes heard to say that the country should be "given back to the blacks", as if, worn out by the ineffectual struggle to prove something that wasn't true, he had finally given up fooling himself. Such statements, like Lawson's story, are meant as jokes, but jokes are often the only way of saying the unsayable.

Australia cannot remain
A land of mystery,
And tainted history,
Of hidden secrets
And eternal regrets.

These lines were written by Matthew Quilty, a direct descendant of the Quiltys who acquired the infamous Bedford Downs Station in 1917. There is only one way to purge the taint, uncover the secret, and ease the otherwise eternal regret, and that is – not to give the country back to the Aborigines because it isn't ours to give – to admit that it has been an Aboriginal country all along.

II

THE BIG IDEA

If you have read thus far it should be clear that my object in writing as a non-Aboriginal Australian addressing other non-Aboriginal Australians is to suggest a way out of the predicament in which we find ourselves as guilty inheritors of a land that was innocently usurped by our ignorant, deluded, desperate forefathers. The single step that begins this journey is the simple admission that ours is an Aboriginal country. All of it. Every single bit. Try saying it to yourself in the mirror. "I live in an Aboriginal country." Even the obvious cannot be recognised as true until somebody says it.

As newcomers to an Aboriginal country, our forefathers should have done their best to assimilate. Instead they took over, leaving the original inhabitants with the duty of assimilation. From first contact the traffic ran the wrong way, towards the impasse in which we now find ourselves. The ignorant presumed to teach the learned, even though they couldn't speak any of the many languages that the learned spoke. The ignorant set about "discovering" a country of which the learned all carried immensely detailed maps in their heads. The ignorant didn't ask the learned which way to go, or how to survive on the track. As a consequence, all of the pioneers suffered and an unknown number of them perished. Unabashed, our forefathers continued their ignorant rampaging. Though they relied heavily on Aborigines in their establishment of the pastoral industry, they never dreamt of consulting them as equals, let alone as their superiors in understanding country, because they were utterly convinced that the most illiterate, uninformed, drunken, down-at-heel European was intellectually and in every other way superior to the blackfella. So the settlers and the squatters were repeatedly wiped out by drought and flood, and the burning of the country was left off. Within a few years banks and corporations had control of virtually all the land, and the pastoralists haven't stopped whingeing since. They planted exotic grasses that would build bigger animals faster. In wildfire such grasses burn too long and too hot, so that the soil heats up and scorches the roots of the old river gums that are the beauty of the inland, so that they too have begun to die. The seeds of buffel grass are nearly as fine and travel as far as smoke; there is nothing we can do now to arrest the process. The traditional custodians of the land hang on, driven hither and yon across the degraded lands and decaying towns of the outback, the dreariest stretches of outer suburbia, and the cacophonous inner cities.

Can it be possible to make a U-turn after two hundred years of careering off in the wrong direction? Can there be any point in admitting at this stage that Australia is an Aboriginal country, when only about 400,000 of the population can claim any Aboriginal descent? Would non-Aboriginal Australians who admit that they are living in an Aboriginal country be doomed to think of themselves as forever aliens in their own birthplace?

Aboriginality is not a matter of blood or genes; Aborigines themselves have to learn Aboriginality. They have to master knowledge of their own country, and of their relationships with neighbouring peoples, and the languages appropriate to trade, negotiation and celebration. Who may learn what is dictated primarily by willingness, evinced in readiness to undergo ordeal in order to be admitted to the deepest secrets, and has nothing to do with colour. It follows that whitefellas can achieve a measure of

Aboriginality and historically they have done. Full-blood white men have been initiated and instructed in the law, and have played their part in the clans.

The second step in the journey is a second statement to the self in the mirror. "I was born in an Aboriginal country, therefore I must be considered Aboriginal." This is a tougher proposition, as long as Aboriginality is thought of as racial, but if we think of Aboriginality as a nationality, it suddenly becomes easier. A man of Algerian descent who is born in France is French; birth and not race is the criterion of nationality. Race is a contested category, perhaps not even a genuine category, and offers no rational basis for the building of a state.

In 1999 indigenous people in the Bega area mounted a public exhibition of cultural artefacts. In the catalogue they explained:

> Because so many of our elders have died over the past years, a lot of this cultural information has been lost, some things have been lost forever … The situation has now reached a critical point where our culture will collapse unless a concerted effort is made now by all people.

The effort to reclaim culture, if it is to be made at all, would result in the acquisition of a measure of Aboriginality, because acquiring Aboriginality is to a large extent the getting of knowledge. Every Aboriginal adult is a teacher; blackfellas will spend huge amounts of time and patience training children in bush lore, kinship relations and ritual observance, or trying by every means in their power to get whitefellas to understand. Aboriginal art is as it were a teaching aid, setting out in mnemonic diagrammatic form the intricate interrelationship of all things, vegetation, landforms, weather, people, events. The first painting at Papunya was a depiction of a dreaming common to the various clan groups who had ended up there, for the edification of their children and anyone else who might have eyes to see. Paddy Jaminji and Rover Thomas made their first series of balga boards to carry in corroborees commemorating recent traumatic events in the realm of the Rainbow Serpent. Having informed their own people they went on to teach the white folks, only to find the white folks buying and selling their work at inflated prices without understanding any of it. Lesser spirits might have given up, but the Aboriginal artists kept painting more and more explicit versions of their reality, constantly modifying their pictorial language and their way of talking about their pictures, waiting in vain for the dawning of comprehension.

The great Emily Kngwarreye, badgered for titles for her works, would always say the one word, "*awelye*", "the lot", "the whole bang lot" even. The charisma of the greatest works being irresistible, whitefellas are now beginning to get the gist of them rather than incessantly trying to translate them; the authority of the patterns is beginning to impress itself upon our brains. Add to that the thousands of Aboriginal people who have abandoned their reticence and sacrificed their privacy to expose their families' trauma and pain, and you will get some idea of how badly they want whitefellas to understand and how hard they are prepared to work at it.

Contrariwise whitefella energies have been directed towards confining and distancing Aboriginality; Paul Hasluck wished "to narrow down the term Australian Aboriginal to mean only those who do not live like Europeans". More recently mining companies have tried to exclude all but Aborigines still living under tribal law from the category Aboriginal, in order to reduce the amount they are committed to pay in royalties. Their latest ruse is to ask the Aboriginal clans themselves to decide who may be considered a member and who not, with predictable results. If the whole country declared itself Aboriginal, the terms of such debates would be turned upside down. Though the debates would not go away they could well involve less stress and confusion for indigenous groups, as the adventurers would have to demonstrate their right to exploit the land rather than the Aborigines having to prove their right to resist such exploitation.

Defining the Aborigine as irrevocably Other has resulted in the creation of non-viable pockets of Aboriginality, human zoos or living museums, in which Aboriginals are considered to be living "unchanged". But Aboriginality is the elaboration of the art of survival and survival demands adaptability. To rethink Aboriginality as inclusive rather than exclusive would not involve the assumption of a phoney ethnicity or the appropriation of the history of any particular Aboriginal people. The owners of specific dreamings would continue to be so still, and would continue to pass them on according to their law as it applies to those concerned. Whitefellas have already learnt to ask permission of traditional owners before entering particular areas; in this they are behaving as Aborigines would behave in the same circumstances. They have also learnt to respect sites that are sacred to others than themselves, just as Aborigines do. Acquired Aboriginality would not entitle whitefellas to assume rights that they don't have now and might encourage them to refrain from taking some of the liberties that they do now.

As Jeremy Beckett observed in his Introduction to *Past and Present: The Construction of Aboriginality*:

> Aboriginality … is a cultural construction. It shares this quality with all other nationalisms, including the Australian, being an example of what Ben Anderson has called "the imagined community". This definition does not imply inauthenticity (it is clear that nationalism, ethnicity and Aboriginality remain some of the most passionately felt forms of identity throughout the word), but simply that they are the products of the human imagination. This is necessarily so because, as Anderson observes, "the members of even the smallest nation will never know most of their fellow-members, meet them, or even hear of them, yet in the minds of each lives the image of their communion". This image is a cultural artefact, achieved by remembering things held in common, but also by strategic forgetting. The "imagining" of communities is not arbitrary, but, like all cultural processes, takes place under particular political and economic circumstances, within a particular cultural tradition and in terms of particular historical experiences. It is these experiences that give the construction its authenticity and also its fluidity.

Aboriginality can hardly be said to exist yet as an imagined community even for black Australians. If it comes into being, rather than perpetuating the phoney divide between so-called white and so-called black, it could as easily encompass both. Neither colour nor genes can explain or justify the gulf that at present yawns between Aboriginal and non-Aboriginal in Australia. As for colour, many of the Aboriginal people I have met are fairer than I am, and as for genes, there is more genetic variation within the Anglo-Celt population than there is genetic difference between Anglo-Celts or any other group within the multicultural mix and the Aborigines. What little difference there might have been has been eroded further by the incorporation of Anglo-Celt genes, as well as Maccassan, Chinese and "Afghan" genes, in the Aboriginal genetic inheritance. In any case genetic difference in itself would not justify stereotyping or discrimination or separation. The road from genes to behaviour is long and the genes involved in behavioural characteristics are scattered throughout the human genome. There is no "gene" for Aboriginality. Aboriginality will come into existence as a consequence of sharing traditions. As Pamela Croft wrote in 2000:

> Always remember that what makes you all Australians is

> the fact that you live on this land, with our ancestral spirits and with our creation stories … what makes you Australian is in fact your interactions with us, the First Nation peoples of this land – in the past, now and in the future. It is what makes you different from your ancestors whose spirits lie in other lands. We are what helps to make you Australian. It is what gives you belonging on and to this land.

Soul-searching about Australian identity has gone on for years without even the glimpse of a resolution. In 1984, Thomas Keneally observed that there was "yet no one such thing as an Australian. The work of defining Australianness … was still in progress". Twenty years later the situation remains unchanged. Australia's only way of branding itself in the world market has been to co-opt the insignia of Aboriginality, with didgeridoos, boomerangs, spot paintings and skeleton animal shapes, which are displayed alongside the Blue Ensign, hardly a happy juxtaposition. Meanwhile Aboriginal art is slowly conquering an uncomprehending world, achieving a visibility that the best whitefella artists can only dream of.

It will be hard for a whitefella to believe that after all that has happened Aboriginal people will allow him to assume

Aboriginality. Any such assumption could well be seen by Aboriginal people as the last and most terrible co-option, a final annihilation. There is a risk, principally a risk of misunderstanding, which mischievous parties on all sides will magnify. Assumed Aboriginality would not allow whitefellas to muscle in on mining royalties or hard-won funding for Aboriginal development and education, but there will be those who will say that it would, just as there were those who said that admitting the justice of Aboriginal land claims would eventually result in wholesale expropriation of owner-occupiers in the suburbs. Admitting Aboriginality would not entitle all Australians to have access to sacred sites – not all Aborigines have access to sacred sites. Indeed, admitting Aboriginality should mean that whitefellas would not consider themselves entitled routinely to defile sacred sites or assume that they have a right of access to what the keepers of the law wish to keep secret. Aboriginal Australians would not think that Uluru is there to be climbed.

III

WHO DOES SHE THINK SHE IS?

My bloodlines are fairly typical of my generation of gubbas. My father was born in Tasmania in 1904; his mother was the granddaughter of two free settlers from Lincolnshire and two convicts. His paternal grandparents were from Ulster. My mother's paternal grandfather was born in the Swiss Ticino and his wife was from Yorkshire; her grandparents on her mother's side were from Ireland and Schleswig-Holstein.

I suppose I am one of those described by Richard Flanagan, winner of a Rhodes Scholarship and a Commonwealth Writers Prize, in an article published in an English newspaper, as "the generation of cultural quislings who fled Australia's shores for England, where they thought they might meet their muse, and ever after berated an Australia they no longer recognised." I don't know who else belongs in this category but, much as I might want to fling the word "quisling" in Flanagan's teeth, I have to admit that if I hadn't been studying in England, if I hadn't been living in the genuinely multicultural society of postgraduate students in Cambridge, I might never have grasped the absurdity of Australians mounting street demonstrations against the South African Springbok Tour in 1971. And might never have glimpsed the Australian situation from an international perspective. When I lived in Australia my condition of unknowing was identical with that described by an older and wiser Mungo MacCallum in his autobiography, *The Man Who Laughs*:

> Of course I knew aborigines existed … Yet I have no conscious memory of ever seeing a black Australian, let alone actually meeting one. I was vaguely aware that they existed somewhere out there in the bush in squalid and primitive conditions and that they were to be pitied as a Stone Age race clearly unable to adapt to Australian civilisation. Yet I remained completely uninterested … I didn't give a stuff about the Australians whose lands had been stolen, whose children had been stolen, whose very existence had been stolen by my ancestors and was still being stolen by my

contemporaries. Okay, so none of this was taught at school and not much of it was known even to contemporary historians at the time. But sheer commonsense and logic should have made it obvious to all but the cretinous that something terrible had happened.

When I came up to Melbourne University, I served on a committee for Aboriginal scholarships, a committee that sat only to record the fact that there were no matriculands eligible for the undergraduate scholarships we were supposed to be awarding. Later, in Sydney, I had glancing acquaintance with the anthropologists Les Hiatt and Mervyn Meggitt. From them I heard rather more about the sexual practices of the desert nomads than about the politics of race in Australia. I knew D'Arcy and Edgar Waters rather better, but I never asked either of them about their Aboriginal inheritance, their 'istory; indeed, though both were intensely interested in Australian folk culture, they seemed uninterested in exploring their own Aboriginality.

It was not until I was half a world away that I could suddenly see that what was operating in Australia was apartheid: the separation and alienation South Africa tried desperately and savagely to impose on their black majority, we had achieved, apparently effortlessly, with our black minority. When I returned to Australia in late 1971, I was determined to see as much as I could of what had been hidden from me. I had to jump the gulf that divided white and black. As soon as it could be arranged I took off for Alice Springs with Roberta Sykes and one other who shall be nameless. When Bobbi explained to the people in the town camp in the Todd River why I was there, they let me camp with them. In the days that followed many of them walked quietly through the deep warm sand to sit with me on my mattress under the river gums, tolerating my insensitive questions, explaining kinship and the laws of avoidance, teaching me far more than I was then able to learn. I could feel all around me a new kind of consciousness in which self was subordinate to *awelye*, the interrelationship of everything, skin, earth, language. Once I realised that, brutalised and badgered as all these people were, their culture was still so strong, I also realised that they would hang on beyond grim death, far beyond the thinning of their bloodlines to invisibility, no matter how intense and relentless the pain. Though Aboriginality can be denied and even forgotten, it cannot cease to exist.

I was with the blackfellas that Saturday night in the beer garden of the Alice Springs Hotel when the police raided it, and I was in the courtroom on Monday morning to see all but one of the people they grabbed receive custodial sentences, some as long as six months, many with hard labour. I knew and the magistrate knew that they had broken no law, but all but one of them pleaded guilty to the charge of drunk and disorderly. They were not represented by any legal counsel. They had received no advice. These were my countrymen, crushed by a legal system that I had been taught at school was the best in the world. I realised that a great deal more work would be needed if I was ever to understand what had gone so terribly wrong. Since then I have inflicted my presence on Yolngu people at Yirrkala, Anmatyerre people at Utopia and Yuendumu, urban Aborigines in Brisbane, Sydney and Melbourne. Over the years I have spent more time with blackfellas than with my own family.

Though I can claim no drop of Aboriginal blood, twenty years ago Kulin women from Fitzroy adopted me. There are whitefellas who insist that blackfellas don't practise adoption; all I can say is that when I asked about the possibility of assuming Aboriginality, the Kulin women said at once, "We'll adopt you." "How do you do that?" I asked, hoping I wouldn't be required to camp in some bleak spot for a month or two, and be painted or smoked or cut about. "That's it," they said. "It's done. We've adopted you." Since then I have sat on the ground with black women and been assigned a skin and taught how to hunt and how to cook shellfish and witchetty grubs, with no worse punishment for getting it wrong than being laughed at.

Even so, after all such encounters, important as they have been to me, I went back to my white world and got on with earning a living, seldom thinking of the Aboriginal people who had been so generous with their time. In her book *Rednecks, Eggheads and Blackfellas*, Gillian Cowlishaw has described how this kind of whitefella behaviour affected her Rembarrnga friends:

> Many visiting nurses and later the resident teachers became familiar, and some formed warm friendships in "their" communities. Despite the shallowness of their incorporation into the framework of kin and country, they were related to not merely as government functionaries but as adopted kin. But they would suddenly depart, often never to be heard of again. "Must have gone back to 'im own country," people would say, with a sense of betrayal or disappointment. ... These encounters were intense experiences and highly valued by both parties, but each side was embroiled in different social institutions which are characterised by different views of human relationships.

Cowlishaw is conscientiously refraining from making a judgment about the superficiality of white relationships with blacks, which should not pre-empt our being struck by the callousness apparent in the whites' easy departures. Contrariwise whitefellas who devote their lives to Aboriginal people not infrequently become extremely possessive, and are bewildered and disappointed when they realise that they mean less to the Aboriginal people than the Aboriginal people mean to them. Nineteenth- and twentieth-century missionaries endured lives of hardship in the outback for love of God; the secular devotees of the twenty-first century are still enacting their own salvation at the expense of the Aborigines, who are prepared to tolerate them only as long as the advantages clearly outweigh the disadvantages. The underlying issue in all such cases is one of control, which Aboriginal Australians have subtly but inexorably resisted. The controllers have acted aggrieved and astonished when apparently co-operative, "civilised" or converted blackfellas have disappeared for months at a time, gone bush, sometimes never to return. The controllers have wrung their hands over the "incorrigibility" of these wayward people, who drift about the country apparently aimlessly, and chuck away the nice clothes, the decent dresses and pinafores that the controllers have given them, apparently unaware that they were obeying a far harsher discipline than anything Christians of any kind might seek to replace it with, in the service of a godhead more pervasive and more immediate than Old Father Whichart.

IV

GOING NATIVE

From first contact the leaders of many Aboriginal peoples saw that sharing of the land would only be possible if the whitefellas could be drawn into the Aboriginal system. They pursued a deliberate policy of co-option, hoping to civilise the invaders who had no conception of a considerate and viable use of country into abandoning their inappropriate concepts of ownership and exclusivity. The most frequently repeated version of the initial attempt at negotiation tells us that the Aborigines upon first seeing white men thought they were their own dead kin "jumped up", that is, resurrected as white men. What was in fact an attempt to classify the white men so that they could function within the dense Aboriginal social fabric is usually treated as a naive conviction literally understood. The whitefella didn't hesitate to exploit what he didn't understand, and helped himself to liberal amounts of loyalty and affection from his black "brother" without considering himself bound in any way by the relationship.

Consider, as a case in point, the relationship between Patrick Durack and his "boys" as told in Mary Durack's most famous work, *Kings in Grass Castles*, which purports to be the story of the Durack men who opened up Cooper's Creek and later the Kimberley. The memoir is based on Patrick Durack's "old account books, stock records, cheque butts, random jottings and letters to his family", buttressed by legal documents and other forms of archival record. Like the plumbing, Aborigines are essential and omnipresent in the narrative but seldom mentioned. When she does expatiate, Durack indulges the tendency noted by Fanon of romanticising the savage, imagining that Aboriginal society was timeless and changeless, which is no more true than that Ned Kelly preceded Captain Cook. Durack offers her own explanation of why the blacks offered no threat to the Irish migrants moving into the Goulburn district in the 1850s.

> Remnants of the proud old tribes of the Tablelands – Mulwarie, Tarlo and Burra-Burra – they watched the

> dreaming of their forefathers lose shape and meaning under the axe and ploughshare of the new people. Gone were the days when they had thought to discourage the newcomers by attacking their shepherds and spearing their stock. They knew themselves beaten now, and the dreamy, changeless philosophy of the old tribes was superseded by a vigorous new way of life of which change was the keynote.

The "vigorous new way of life" introduced by the white man has left the outback studded with ghost towns while the Aboriginality that Durack saw floating helplessly off into the past endures.

When Patrick Durack acquired a farm and a cattle-run in the Goulburn district, the Aborigines came to hang out there.

> The new settlers found their dark-skinned visitors good-humoured and amusing, even helpful in a desultory fashion, until a whim seized them and they were on their way.

In 1863 a whim seized Patsy Durack and he too was on his way, droving stock into western Queensland where he hoped to take up a much bigger tract of land. Near the Kyabra Creek the travellers got into difficulties and were rescued by a "party of blacks".

> The women wore armlets of possum skin, necklets of clustered kangaroo teeth or small human bones – relics of drought-born babies, killed and eaten to be born again, they reasoned, in better times … Astonishingly one spoke a few words of garbled English and was later found to have been in contact with King, the sole survivor of Burke's party of two years before.

Just as they had for King, the blacks found and cooked food for the drovers, and earnestly urged them to turn back. When the whitefellas persisted in their misconceived endeavour, the blacks disappeared, apparently leaving them to their fate. Only when they had killed their last horse to drink from its jugular vein did the drovers finally decide to turn back, to find the blacks, who had known all along where they were, ready to help them again, feeding them and showing them the rockholes where sweet water might be found. This generosity and forbearance is recorded without comment. There is no sense of mutuality or any reciprocal obligation on the part of the whitefellas.

In 1867 Durack set off again with his family, and the black family of a "young fellow" known to white posterity simply as "Soldier". Other "native riders" were "in sole command" of the cattle and horses, but they are nameless. At Mobel Creek, Soldier's wife's country, Soldier was sent ahead to negotiate with the Aborigines, who would be given beef if they refrained from spearing the stock.

> One good-humoured grizzle-haired fellow with a bone through his nose and a body ornate with tribal scars at once attached himself to [Durack] and was given, along with the name of Cobby, a shirt and trousers, a hat and a pair of stockmen's boots.

Why an initiated man of the "Murragon" people (who are nowadays called Maranganji, in various spellings) would choose to become "Mr Durack's boy" is not a question that interests Mary Durack, though to any understanding of the whole situation it would appear to be critical. Later we are told that Cobby had been the ambassador or message-stick carrier to the neighbouring "Boontamurra" (nowadays Punthamara), which suggests that he originally joined Durack's party in a similar capacity as some kind of permanent negotiator for his people with the white man. Two large groups of Aborigines came to beg meat at Durack's cattle camp at Mobel Creek, which suggests that there may have been a severe shortage of food at the time. Meanwhile Soldier and another Aboriginal called Scrammy Jimmy helped Durack's brother-in-law to round up 200 clean-skin horses and drive them 800 miles to the saleyards in Port Augusta where they fetched good prices. When Durack moved onward into Queensland he was guided by Cobby who found food and water for him and introduced him to the "wild" Punthamara, owners of the land he eventually took up at Thylungra. There Durack was saluted by Burrakin, an initiated man of the Punthamara.

> "Him yabber you brother belong him," Cobby said. "Long time him brother die. Now him jump up whiteman."

Durack, who believed that Aborigines were "kindly and childlike savages", accepted Burrakin and his two brothers into his retinue, altering his name to Pumpkin. His brothers he named Melon Head and Kangaroo. Dame Mary gives no hint as to why three Punthamara men should cast their lot with the white interloper. Nor does she tell us until much later that the "boy" Pumpkin was married by law to an older woman. Cobby, Soldier and Scrammy Jimmy joined the Punthamara "boys" at Thylungra, where sometimes as many as 600 "natives" camped. When Durack's brother-in-law took it upon himself to marry two young people who were of the wrong skins and allowed them to camp in his saddle shed, his temerity cost Soldier his life. To keep the newlyweds safe from the reprisal that he knew must follow, Soldier laid his swag across the doorway of the saddle shed where he was beheaded by the Aborigines who came looking for the errant couple. Soldier's loyalty was replicated by Scrammy Jimmy. When the station owner went looking for Soldier's murderers and was stunned by a flung stone, Scrammy Jimmy split the head of one of his assailants with his tomahawk. During the tense times that followed Cobby and his wife slept in their swags across the doorway of the homestead, ready to raise the alarm at the first sign of trouble. Dame Mary seems to take the loyalty of these Aborigines to the Durack family as a compliment to her own kind, never asking herself what considerations might have moved the Maraganji men to risk their lives for the white interloper.

To a reader who does not identify with whitefellas, the Durack saga remains a story untold. The agents who understand the full context of the events are mute. The blacks make difficult decisions but we are not privy to them. They risk their lives and we have no notion why. When the Duracks' stupendous land-grab resulted in a series of holdings registered in various names, in all some 3000 square miles, Pumpkin, "right hand boy" of the conquering Durack, was still living in a humpy.

In 1881 Durack was seized by another whim, this time to divest himself of Thylungra and help himself to a large slice of the Kimberley. When he prepared to move his family into Brisbane, Pumpkin asked "earnestly" if he might not come with them. Durack "held to his belief that even so exceptional a native would fret and sicken away from his own country". Pumpkin, by now a widower, returned to "his lonely humpy". Later, when Durack decided to travel overland to see the Kimberley property for himself, Pumpkin went with him and helped him to build the homestead at Argyle, where once more he guarded his master from a night attack by the "Mirriwun" (nowadays Miriuwung, in the usual galaxy of spellings) by sleeping on the verandah. "Pumpkin was the mainstay of the station on Behn River. Stockman, horse-tailer, blacksmith, butcher, gardener and general handyman, he gave for love and pride of being a good man, of everything he had." Though Durack presumes to account for Pumpkin's motives, she never tells us, presumably because she doesn't know, how old Pumpkin is, not even when he introduces a "shy, young girl" from the Ord River people as his wife, to help the new missus in the house. The unusual arrangement ends in tragedy seven years later, when Pumpkin's wife is speared in the leg, and an older woman is fatally wounded. For Dame Mary these are not events worth dwelling on, though they are more terrible and dramatic than anything that happened to her hero. After Durack lost his wife he felt "that only Pumpkin still believed in him". On his deathbed in 1898 Durack's last words were, "Tell Pumpkin to fetch up the horses, Mary. I am ready now." To Pumpkin, the "best friend" he "ever had", he left the pocket watch his wife gave him on their wedding day.

Kings in Grass Castles could have been the story of a lifelong friendship between a black man and a white man, but it isn't. Though Durack and some of her informants are full of praise for Pumpkin's faithfulness and his intelligence, they are no more interested in his personality than if he had been an exceptional dog. For Durack's granddaughter, Pumpkin is merely a mirror in which she sees reflected the indomitable superiority of the white man whose powerful influence enabled this savage to transcend himself. Patrick Durack probably realised that Pumpkin, who was physically more agile and adept than he and better at handling horses and cattle than he, who spoke many languages and understood the bush a thousand times better than he, who was capable of risking his life repeatedly for his friend and uninterested in any reward, was actually his superior, without whose help he would have accomplished nothing. More than once he realised that Pumpkin was feigning deafness so that he could safely ignore a stupid command and he admitted more than once that it was Pumpkin who really ran Thylungra. Nevertheless, Pumpkin does not even have his own entry in the index to *Kings in Grass Castles*, which is not so much Durack's fault as that of her editors.

There are dozens, even hundreds of other blacks in the Durack story. Of Michael Durack's offsider Black Willie, the Larrakia men Pintpot and Pannikin, one-eyed Jimmie, his gin Susan, little Waddi Mundoai with his wooden leg, Cherry, Davey, Billy, Sultan, Tommy, Charlie, "that flash abo Pompey", Ulysses, Maggie, Boxer, Dick, Aled Meith or Meid, Barney and Nipper we know little more than their names; in this saga of the heroic endeavour of the white man, the hordes of "wild" blacks who struggled to prevent the invasion of the Kimberley and paid with their lives are no more than shadows on the backdrop.

The ultimate purpose of a book like *Kings in Grass Castles* is to elevate the squattocracy, deservedly loathed by the Aussie battler, to heroic status. In such hagiography rank opportunists are credited with "courage" and "vision" rather than simple greed and land-hunger. Ironically the Duracks came from the lowest of the low, at least in the estimation of British landowners, for they were aboriginal Irish, also known as "black", "bog" or "wild" Irish. Their attempts to protect their country and religion had been represented by the Protestant elite in the same contemptuous manner as the struggles of black Australians would be by the colonial elite, but victims of racist oppression are slow to recognise when they are acting oppressively in their turn. Instead they try to make common cause with the oppressor. Durack talks of her forebears' family holding sway in ancient times and interprets all flattering references to knightly O'Dubraic, O'Durack and Du Roc families as if they were historical fact and about her family. What is undeniable is that Mary Durack was descended from landless and illiterate peasants who attempted to improve their wretched situation by gambling and brewing poteen. Her Durack great-grandparents came to Australia in 1849 as indentured labour. As soon as they accumulated spare cash they began to ape the manners of their old oppressors, decking their tables with damask and silver. However, they retained their brand of superstitious Catholicism; Michael

Durack carried a "holy" relic with him at all times and was distressed when he lost it. (Needless to say it was Pumpkin who found it for him.) Patrick Durack, known as "Boonari" to "his" Aboriginal workforce, may have been less bloodthirsty than other settlers, who thought nothing of killing blacks, but his reluctance to ill-treat his "boys" seems after all to have been of the same order as his reluctance to mistreat animals.

> Even the blacks moved briskly on Thylungra for, paternal though he was, Boonari's quick impatience was something to look out for. It is said he once stamped an indelible 7PD brand on a slow-moving black rump, a distinguishing mark that the boy wore proudly till the day of his death!

The tell-tale "It is said" that prefixes this repellent observation shows that oral sources might have given a different account of Boonari's ways of dealing with "his boys" than could be found in Dame Mary's archival sources. Dame Mary had clearly not seen the brand for herself, nor had she any way of verifying the Aboriginal man's pride in having been so marked.

Australians conscious of their own Aboriginality would not rewrite *Kings in Grass Castles* from the point of view of

Cobby or Pumpkin. To do so would involve unbearable appropriations like Douglas Lockwood's *I, the Aboriginal*, in which the white author takes it upon himself to assume the persona of Waipuldanya or Wadjiri-Wadjiri of the Alawa people, otherwise known as Phillip Roberts, the first full-blood Aborigine to be granted citizenship with his family in 1960. Lockwood's book probably did more than most to familiarise whitefellas with the facts of Alawa life, but the exercise involved a take-over of Waipuldanya's personality, and a distortion of his point of view, not to mention excruciatingly bad writing.

> My mother, Nora, wore a simple lap-lap. Her breasts were bare, heavily laden with the latent milk which would soon feed an infant brother. Her long black hair flew unconcernedly, untended, in the breeze.

This is supposed to be the unprompted observation of a seven-year-old Aboriginal boy living on the Roper River Mission in about 1929. Lockwood's book is an interesting if largely unconscious exercise in juggling multiple identities, but his is not a road that can be taken in the twenty-first century. What is accessible to us is a more intelligent reading of our own myths. We need to see through the obfuscatory detail to the blackness underneath, and interpret the truth that lurks beneath the self-congratulatory rhetoric of the frontier epic.

The intimate but unequal relationship between Patrick Durack and Pumpkin was nothing new; it had been replicated time and again ever since Bennelong befriended Governor Phillip. Tim Flannery's way of writing about this relationship in his introduction to *The Birth of Sydney* (1999) suggests that a change in our perception of such events has already happened.

> It is clear to me that the Eora did not view themselves as inferior to the Europeans in any way, and thus saw no reason to adopt their ways. It is not hard to imagine why, for early Sydney was a degenerate settlement, full of violent, starving and often immoral people. This must have been obvious to the Eora, many of whom – including Bennelong, a leading Eora whose name means "great fish" – considered themselves to be distinctly superior to the Europeans in everything that mattered, including hunting, fighting and managing the land. Indeed, the superior intellects and morality of many Eora were evident even to some European observers such as Watkin Tench. Late in 1789 Bennelong ... was kidnapped by the

> Europeans, who wished to open relations with the Eora … Bennelong, though at first enraged, took advantage of the opportunity his captivity afforded him and became a favourite of Governor Phillip and the other leading Europeans.

Before Bennelong another Eora known to history as Arabanoo had exerted himself to win the trust of the governor only to die of smallpox in 1789. Arabanoo and Bennelong are just two of the many blackfellas who came more than half-way to build a relationship with the invaders of their country, often leaving behind family and country to accompany their new kinsman wherever his wandering should lead them, only to be abandoned or sent home when their classificatory brother, who imagined himself their master, abandoned them. It was not until after his bridge-building had failed that Bennelong's behaviour became belligerent and he was classed "a most insolent and troublesome savage".

Sometimes it was women who were meant to provide the ties that would weave the newcomers into the fabric of Aboriginal society. So Patyegarang became the language teacher, and probably the lover, of Governor Phillip's lieutenant William Dawes. When the Palawa elder Mannarlargenna yielded his daughter to the sealer George Briggs in 1808, he had every reason to expect Briggs to accept his position within the kinship network. By 1830 seventy-four women of Aboriginal and Maori descent are recorded as living with sealers on the islands in Bass Strait; though many of them had been abducted, raped and forced to gather and prepare food for their masters, others had not. George Augustus Robinson's determination to round up the Aborigines was driven as much by a desire to protect white society from the black as the other way about. How successful he was may be deduced by the fact that between 1800 and 1830 sixty-nine half-caste children were born on the islands in Bass Strait. When their Aboriginal wives were caught up in Robinson's dragnet, the sealers often refused to allow their children to go with them to the settlements; in this they showed far more attachment to them than later settlers on the mainland would do, but then children of any colour were in demand in the colony principally as an unwaged labour force.

Relationships between Aboriginal and white women are probably even more important than those with men in working a leaven of Aboriginality into Australian society. Black gins smoothed the birthing pillow of the white woman, and nursed both mother and child. Aboriginal women worked alongside the missus from dawn till dusk, and were intimately involved in the socialisation of her children. The children of the missus and the station servants played together, until the awful moment when the white child's feet were crammed into shoes and he was sent off to school. Such female friendships were to prove no more durable or egalitarian than those between white man and black man. However affectionate they might have been, they were brusquely truncated when circumstances changed. In *Broken Circles: Fragmenting Indigenous Families 1800–2000*, Anna Haebich tells how Lady Franklin, wife of the first governor of Tasmania, took on Mathinna, the orphaned five-year-old daughter of the leader of the Port Davey people, and kept her as an exotic human pet. Lady Franklin liked to be seen in public attended by this little dark figure, resplendent in a vivid red gown with a possum curled around her neck. When time came to return to England Lady Franklin dumped Mathinna in the orphanage and forgot all about her. In *The Last Tasmanians* (1973), D. Davies quotes from the Hobart *Mercury*:

> Poor Mathinna was transferred sobbing and broken-hearted, from the tender care of one who had always proved far more than a mother to her, and the luxury and

> grandeur of Government House, to a cold stretcher in the dormitory of the Queen's asylum. She soon fell sick and was taken to a bed in the Hospital, she had no friends.

Having alienated the child from her people and their way of life, Lady Franklin then imposed upon her a life sentence of self-determination. Mathinna was released from the orphanage in 1851 and returned to Oyster Cove. How she was meant to survive is not apparent; she apparently resorted to prostitution and alcohol, and met her death not long after by drowning.

When Edna Eckford Quilty went out as a raw young bride to Lansdowne in 1952, the black women not only took care of all the housework for her but, rather than leave her on her own in the rudimentary dwelling at the homestead, took her foraging with them, taught her where to find sugar bag, how to track and kill a goanna, how to breathe underwater; they played games with her "naked and free in the water" and took special care of her when they knew before she did that she was pregnant. None of this intimacy entitled them to friendship. They knew all about Quilty but she knew next to nothing about them. In her memoir *Nothing Prepared Me!* she supplies no information about any of her "faithful old lubras", or the clan-group they belonged to or its past vicissitudes. The Aboriginal population on Lansdowne is divided simply into "our" blacks and "wild" blacks. Yet Quilty is aware of a different reality; speaking of half-castes she says, "Many have been sired [*sic*] by some of our most prominent and respected citizens."

We will never know just how many of the founders of the pastoral industry in remote Australia lived with Aboriginal women and had children by them. Quilty evidently knows but is not saying. Sometimes the whitefellas married the mother of their children, but not if they had pretensions to becoming "prominent" and "respected". Usually they left their half-caste children to grow up with their mothers in the blackfellas' camp, and used them as cheap labour – if they survived. Some even boasted that as well as cattle they were breeding their own labour force. The Aborigines accepted the yella-fella children, and incorporated them in the kinship system, and would have accepted their white fathers too if they had been willing to be classed as Aboriginal.

As we know from Sally Morgan's memoir *My Place*, for nine years Alfred Howden Drake-Brockman, owner of Corunna Downs Station in the Pilbara, shared two Aboriginal women with their Aboriginal husband. Bindiding, whitefella name Ginnie, bore him a son, Albert; her co-wife,

Annie, bore him a son, Arthur, and a daughter, Daisy. Drake-Brockman acknowledged none of them. When his half-caste children were christened they were given the surname "Corunna". Daisy Corunna told her grand-daughter, Sally Morgan:

> Now some people say my father wasn't Howden Drake-Brockman, they say he was this man from Malta. What can I say? I never heard about this man from Malta … aah, you see that's the trouble with us blackfellas, we don't know who we belong to. No one'll own up …

Daisy knew of other whitefellas whose children grew up in the blackfellas' camp on Corunna Station:

> There was Peter Linck, the well-sinker. I think he was German; he lived at the outcamp. He had Rosie, not my sister Rosie, another one. Then there was Fred Stream, by jingoes, there was a few kids that belonged to him. He had Sarah, her children were really fair, white blackfellas, really.
>
> Aah, that colour business is a funny thing. Our colour goes away. You mix us with the white man, and pretty soon, you got no blackfellas left. Some of these whitefellas you see walking around they really black underneath.

There are many blackfellas in the Pilbara who could trace their parentage back to Lang Hancock, but none of them is represented in the interminable lawsuits over whether Hancock's third wife or the daughter of his second wife should get the bulk of his fortune, most of which is income derived from selling iron ore which was not morally Hancock's to sell in the first place, being the heritage of the families of the women who bore his piccaninnies. None of the lawyers who have been making a good living over the division of the Hancock spoils has tried to bring an action on behalf of Hancock's Aboriginal descendants, there being no way for British law to recognise a moral claim in the absence of legal entitlement.

Aboriginal reticence made matters much easier for the whitefellas. Even now blackfellas will not expatiate on past relationships between white men and black women and will not discuss the inheritance of particular individuals, even though everyone in the community knows the truth. White men preferred black partners because they could dump them and their children with impunity; there was no likelihood of a paternity suit, or of a dark woman and her blond children turning up to disrupt a church wedding with a white woman of good family. What the Aboriginal women offered (in those relatively rare instances where they were not actually raped) was a genuine, affectionate, non-possessive connection which the white men ultimately spurned. Why and how they found it so easy to ignore their own children growing up in the black encampments only yards away from where they lived and worked remains for me at least a mystery.

The Aboriginal people were no more likely to wander into any of these relationships with white folks than they were to wander aimlessly from place to place. All their actions were purposeful; it was the whitefella in his boundless ignorance who characterised Aborigines as childish, spontaneous and irrational as a way of excluding the possibility that that they may have had more rational aims and more discipline in pursuing them than he did. Like an irresponsible child, the whitefella had sex with women whose children he didn't want and told himself that the people who were exercising the role of parents were the ones who were childish. Instead of claiming their children by Aboriginal women and so providing them with a white identity, whitefellas preferred to set up orphanages and asylums where Aboriginality would be starved and beaten out of them. It didn't work. The lost generations returned to haunt white Australians with the crime of their forefathers, which was not to beget them, though there was rape as well as love in the business, so much as it was to reject them. White society continues to devise ways of spurning or discounting the proffered intimacy, the push to a meaningless "self-determination" being one of the latest of a series of mutually contradictory and internally incoherent policy initiatives, to be followed by the meaningless and therefore acceptable notion of "reconciliation".

For 200 years the Aboriginal peoples have been seducing the whitefellas, subtly drawing them into their web of dreams, and though the whitefellas struggle and protest, they are being drawn inexorably closer. From the day of the first contact the blackfellas were never very far away and now are closer to us than ever. We yelp with surprise when a popular talk-show host is revealed to have 'istory, as blackfellas say, but we should have guessed. The black communities are bound to us by a multitude of blood ties which it is vain for us to deny, but we are blinded by denial and its companion, guilt.

One of Henry Lawson's least popular stories, seldom reprinted and seldom chosen as a school text, appears in *Over the Sliprails* (1900). It's called "Black Joe", and is a rare instance of a Lawson story in which Aborigines play a major part. Usually if a black Australian appears at all in a Lawson story, it is as a background figure, a splendid native policeman at a railway station, the occasional "old black gin" called in to deliver a white woman's child, or a collection of bones. "Black Joe" is about the relationship between two boys, Black Joe, son of Black Jimmie, and White Joe. The boys met when White Joe was visiting his uncle's station, where Black Jimmie was employed as a shepherd and "lived in a gunyah on the rise at the back of the sheep-yards". White Joe, who is also the narrator, remembers:

> I liked Black Jimmie very much and would willingly have adopted him as a father. I should have been quite content to spend my days in the scrub, enjoying life in dark and savage ways, and my nights "alonga possum rug"; but the family had other plans for my future.

The two Joes find themselves in trouble for different reasons …

> Joe and I discussed existence at a waterhole down the creek next afternoon, over a billy of crawfish we had boiled and a piece of gritty damper, and decided to retire beyond the settled districts – some five hundred miles or so – to a place Joe said he knew of … I thought I might as

> well start and be a blackfellow at once, so we got a rusty pan without a handle, and cooked about a pint of fat yellow oak-grubs; and I was about to fall to, when we were discovered … I was sent home and Joe went droving with uncle soon after that, else I might have lived a life of freedom and died out peacefully with the last of my adopted tribe.

Soon after, Black Joe dies on the track, of tuberculosis. White Joe cannot tell his white relatives what this bereavement means to him and spends a good deal of time hiding behind the pigsty nursing his secret grief.

What is fascinating about this story is that it is a fantasy of going native, even though to do so is understood to be a death sentence, as Lawson or his narrator states categorically that blacks die out, "one by one when brought within the ever-widening circle of civilisation". Though it is almost certain to be shorter, native life is understood to be superior to "civilisation", especially as White Joe's uncle is another rural failure, a victim of "drought and depression, and foot rot and wool-rings, and overdrafts and bank owners". Lawson is clearly guilty of romanticising blackfella life in this story, but he also shows an awareness of Aboriginal culture that was unusual in popular writers at the time.

White Joe's dream of escape into hunter-gathererdom was the administrators' nightmare; mainstream culture was terrified of the appeal of the possum rug.

V

COULD WE GET AWAY WITH IT?

A few years ago a group of blackfellas came to England and planted a flag on the beach at Dover, claiming the land for the Aboriginal nation. The event was laughed off, by which token the British should be prepared to laugh off their own absurd attempt at annexation of Australia in 1770. Our concern should not be whether the British would accept a Unilateral Declaration of Independence from us, because in fact they would have no more choice in this instance than they did in the case of Rhodesia, but whether the Aborigines will allow white Australians to make common cause with them. Some may not, and we may have to consider the establishment of autonomous Aboriginal republics within the continent, with whitefella-style boundaries and passports and what-have-you, a situation which in some respects already exists. Such discrete areas are proving very hard for Aborigines to live in, for reasons that to discuss would be to go far beyond my brief; some are historic, while others have to do with the changes that have been wrought within Aboriginal society over the last 200 years. If Australia were to own up to its Aboriginality, the Aboriginal communities that have been sectioned off, imprisoned on their own land as it were, could re-enter the mainstream and take on the cosmopolitan character they had of old, when they traded with, and fought with, and intermarried with their neighbours.

More vexing is the question of whether blackfellas would let us become Aboriginal, whether they would adopt us. This is not a decision I can pre-empt; neither is it a decision any one group can make on behalf of all the others. The signs however are hopeful. It is not in the least surprising that Aborigines should have attacked newcomers to their country; what is surprising is the number of examples where first contact was friendly, co-operative and even protective. In 1797 David Collins recorded the case of the escaped convict James Wilson who after "herding with savages in different parts of the country" and being scarified on shoulders and breast turned up again in Sydney wearing nothing but a kangaroo-skin apron. The authorities were sure that if he were to be sentenced to indentured labour again, his "savage" allies would spirit him away once more. Thirty years later the convict George Clarke absconded and fled northwards to Liverpool Plains, where he was taken in and helped by the Kamilaroi. To avoid capture he painted himself black. He was eventually initiated, took two wives and became a senior law-man.

Walter Smith, Australian bushman, eponymous hero of R.G. Kimber's *Man from Arltunga*, born in 1893, was the great-grandson of an Arabana woman from the Peake area in northern SA who bore a daughter, Mary, to an unknown white man, probably a member of one of John McDougall Stuart's expeditions in about 1860. In about 1875 Mary gave birth to a daughter, Topsy, whose father, an Oodnadatta police officer, did not acknowledge her. Later Mary took up with another white man called Arthur Evans and lived and worked with him at the Alice Well store and then on the Arltunga goldfield. Then he too abandoned her and returned to the Peake area where he married a white woman. Mary went to live with her daughter Topsy who had married a Welsh miner and stayed with her till her death. Topsy's eleven children had no great share of Aboriginal genes but they lived among the Arrernte and learned their language and their ways.

> They learnt by observation, practice and encouragement, those things that were to be of use to them in their later lives. In particular they learnt to read the sky and the land, to know the wind clouds and the rain-clouds, to gather bush-tucker such as bush-bananas, wild passionfruit, wild oranges, yelka bulbs, yams, blood-wood apples and native-figs and to read the tracks of animals ranging in size from insects to rock wallabies and hill-kangaroos.

In about 1905, when Walter Smith was watching a Pitjantjatjara law-man carving a tjurunga, he was told that when he was older and had "become a man" by tribal law, he would be taught the law. The fact that he was seven-eighths white presented no obstacle. It was not until 1924 that Walter was initiated by Joe Brown, one of three white men who had gone through the law, in a camp of 400 Pitjantjatjara men celebrating the Rain and Red Ochre ceremonies. In the years that followed he underwent further painful rituals to become in his turn a senior law-man.

Historically Aborigines have put a huge amount of effort into building connections with whitefellas. The relationship they tried to build with the whites was a relationship of equals, with shared access to food, water and women. Whether they were saving the life of some fool explorer or an escaped convict or a child lost in the bush, the blacks didn't use their superiority in the situation to exact tribute or recompense or to exert control. They didn't flog or hang people who acted in ways they regarded as criminal, but speared them man to man. Regardless of the services performed for the white man by the black man, regardless of the degree of intimacy in the relationship, the white man always abandoned his black mate and returned to his all-white enclave. It's late now to try to reverse the trend, late for the gubba to move towards the blackfella, but we shall never know if it is indeed too late if we don't make the effort.

VI

WHAT'S IN A NAME?

From the first contact, whitefellas had difficulty in naming black Australians. At first they called them "Indians" or "natives". By 1873, according to Trollope, the word "native" was "almost universally applied to white colonists born in Australia" and the people who lived in the country before the advent of the white man were usually described as "aborigines" with or without a capital. The *Oxford English Dictionary* defines "aborigines" as "a purely Latin word, applied to those who were believed to have been the inhabitants of any country *ab origine*, i.e., from the beginning". The word was applied to ethnic groups in Italy, Greece, Britain, Germany, India and Africa long before it was applied to the original inhabitants of Australia. Only in the case of Australia did the word "aboriginal" persist as the official designation for all the pre-colonial inhabitants, and now it is usually capitalised, as if it referred to a nationality. As the appellation "Aboriginal" admits that the people referred to are the original inhabitants it would seem to be preferable to the often-used alternative "Indigenous" or "indigene" or even "indigine" (*sic*), which are simply other ways of saying "native".

Administrators who dubbed black Australians "Aborigines" can never have believed that Australia was "terra nullius" for the very word refutes such a claim. People who now try to argue that Aboriginal Australians are not really aboriginal because they came from somewhere else 50,000 years ago are grasping at straws. There is no limitation of territory or race in the word "aboriginal", which is a historical term applicable to all and any groups present before colonisation. It therefore applies to Torres Strait Islanders every bit as much as it does to Tasmanians, and yet in official nomenclature Torres Strait Islanders are singled out as if they had no claim to have been present before colonisation.

One peculiarity of the word "aborigines" is that in Latin it is always plural; the singular "aborigine" is formed by treating the Latin as if it were an English plural and simply taking the "s" off to form a singular. It is thought by some that the word "aborigine" is in some sense pejorative or discriminatory, and generally there is confusion about whether it might not be preferable to use the adjective "aboriginal" as if it were a noun, or to couple the adjective with a noun as in "Aboriginal people". Such linguistic pussyfooting is symptomatic of a deep unease that pervades the thinking of white Australians about Australian blacks. Even the word "black" used to cause a frisson, and for a few years the euphemism "coloured" appeared in genteel parlance. White Australians are in the main anxious to avoid upsetting black Australians by referring to them in ways that they might find offensive, but at the same time they are so unfamiliar with black people that they have no way of knowing what gives offence and what doesn't. A minority, who still use the contemptuous abbreviation "abo", just don't give a damn.

Any effort on the part of whitefellas to avoid lumping all the Aboriginal peoples together under the same name seems doomed to failure. Most whitefellas cannot differentiate between one Aboriginal group and another. Australian schoolchildren are more likely to be able to name native American peoples than Australian. Whitefella experts have never succeeded in arriving at a manageable convention for rendering the names of Australian Aboriginal peoples. Are the nomads of the Simpson Desert to be called Aranda, Aranta, Arunta or Arrernte? In learned journals all four versions of the name can be found in a single article. Transliteration that attempts to provide a surer guide to Aboriginal speech-sounds results in words that whitefellas find impossible to pronounce or remember. The intervention of the academics, who commandeer certain peoples and language groups and subject them to intense scrutiny, with the ultimate aim of being accepted by their peers as the experts in their chosen subject, has had the unintended effect of forcing black and white further apart. Though no one would nowadays use the word "savage" to describe Aboriginal Australians, academic versions of blackness present it as so complex, so exotic and so irrevocably "other" that whitefellas can excuse themselves from making any effort to understand it.

Recently, more accessible designations for Aboriginal peoples have come into currency, in part in response to views like those of Mudrooroo Nyoongah that "The term Aboriginal or Aborigine is a white imposition on the indigenous peoples of Australia." Mudrooroo prefers to be designated Nyoongah, which is itself an alternative spelling of Nyungar, a word meaning "person" in a group of Aboriginal languages. In Victoria and much of New South

Wales, "Koori" or "Koorie" is the preferred term, while in southern and central Queensland it is "Murri" or "Mari" and in northern Queensland "Bama", around Kalgoorlie "Mulbara", in the Pilbara "Mulba", around the Murchison River "Wongi", in Arnhem Land "Yolngu", in Central Australia "Anangu", on the south coast of New South Wales "Yuin" and so forth.

As Mudrooroo explains, "Being a Nyoongah means something different to being an 'Aboriginal' – we're a mix of races who belong to the south-west of Western Australia." Aboriginal groups in South Australia also call themselves Nyoongah or "Nunga". Such names are not the names of "tribes" nor do they correspond to language groups. Whitefellas using such terms, which might be thought of as meaning something like "our mob", might well feel guilty of over-familiarity and even of appropriation; they are also quite likely to use them for the wrong people. Aboriginality would involve trying, not to join one or other of these vaguely defined groups, but to participate in the imagined community that overarches them all. In Aboriginal languages people use different names to describe themselves in different contexts; arriving at acceptable single names by which groups of clans sharing some elements of culture as well as connections to a particular region may be known to outsiders is yet another example of Aboriginal peoples' unceasing effort to make themselves understandable to people with no interest in understanding them.

The generic names do not always sit easily; Aboriginal interclan relationships have been the subject of negotiations that have continued over aeons, and sometimes involved stand-offs and conflict. Such matters become more, not less important after a catastrophe like the mortality that followed white contact at the beginning of the nineteenth century and again after the influenza epidemic of 1918. The elaborate kinship systems that characterise all hunter-gatherer groups require optimum populations in order to function; when those populations fall below a certain level, new, often strained and uneasy, relationships must be forged in a hurry. The black communities that came up against the white settlers were reacting to pressure that could at any moment cause their implosion or disintegration. The emergence of the new names for clusters of indigenous groups is further evidence of the same pressure towards implosion and the erosion of separateness as a principle of organisation in Aboriginal societies.

"Aboriginal" is certainly not a designation blackfellas have chosen for themselves but it describes something that before contact they had no need to name, the collectivity of all the black nations on the island continent and off-shore. The Aborigines may not call themselves that, but the Germans don't call themselves Germans, the French French, or the Dutch Dutch. These labels, like the Aboriginal label, are all English names for non-English people. It is not a sign that English-speakers despise the French that they call Bourgogne Burgundy, and mispronounce Paris and Rheims, or that they consider themselves superior to the Italians by calling their most famous cities Rome, Florence, Venice, Milan, Turin instead of their Italian names. The fact that white Australians feel so squeamish about adapting Aboriginal names so that they can pronounce them is further evidence of their lack of faith in their own motives. The whole Aboriginal question ends up consigned to the too-hard basket, and there we are content to let it stay.

Our settler ancestors showed no such sensitivity. Within months of the arrival of the first fleet Aboriginal words entered the language. Every Australian schoolchild ought to know that Captain Cook named the kangaroo in 1770, saying that *Macropus giganteus* was called "kangooroo" or "kanguru" by the "natives" of the Endeavour River region in Queensland. The subsequent history of the word is typical of whitefella interaction with the complexity of Aboriginal culture. On the one hand it was claimed that the same word was used (for a different species of *Macropus*) in Tasmania, but that the word used in Port Jackson (for yet another member of the genus) was "patagorong" or something like it. Every Australian Aboriginal language would have had a specific word for every *Macropus* species endemic in their areas, as well as different words for adults, juveniles, males and females within the various species. If Aborigines all over Australia came to use the generic word "kangaroo" it is because they learnt it to communicate with whitefellas. The latest wisdom is that our word "kangaroo" derives from Guugu Yimithirr "gangurru", which designates the animal known to zoologists as *Macropus robustus* and not *Macropus giganteus.* Koala, the vernacular name of *Phascolarctos cinereus,* is supposed to be derived from "kulla" in Dippil, "kula" on George's River. "Dingo", "warrigul", "corroboree", "myall", "coee", "gibber" and "gin" meaning "woman" are all words from the Dharuk language spoken around Port Jackson. "Bung" as in "going bung", "dilly" as in "dilly bag", "humpy", "currawong" and "jackeroo" are all derived from the Jagara language spoken around Brisbane. In dictionaries of Australian English many other words are described as derived from a language called simply "ab." Or "probably ab." As linguistic adepts, blackfellas learnt new words almost as soon as they heard them; within a very few years some of the white man's locutions were being repeated in the farthest reaches of the continent, words transferred from other colonies, "piccaninny", "goanna" and "barracuda" from the Spanish West Indies, "bandicoot" from the name of an Indian pig-rat, "emu" a Portuguese name applied to any of a number of large bird species. Now-forgotten Aboriginal languages survive as linguistic fossils, words like "lubra", which is possibly Tasmanian, "billabong", from Wiradhuri perhaps, "budgeree" meaning "good", "bale" meaning "no", "yan" meaning "go", "cabon" meaning "much", "wombat", "boomerang", thought by some to be a Nyungar word, and "didgeridoo".

The matrix language of the colony was pidgin, a language created quick-time by the Aborigines specifically to communicate with the white men who had taken control of their world. The very existence of this language, now called Kriol, is further evidence of the Aborigines' struggle to make themselves understood. White settlers didn't just fail to learn any Aboriginal language, they didn't trouble themselves to teach correct English to the blacks who worked alongside them either. Kriol was the result of Aborigines organising English nouns and verbs within Aboriginal syntactic systems. Whitefellas could understand it though they were about as unlikely to speak it to other whitefellas as to give up chairs and sit on the ground. Typically, by speaking Kriol blackfellas allowed whitefellas to continue to occupy their fantasy space above rather than alongside them.

The first whitefellas to familiarise themselves to any extent with an Aboriginal language were the missionaries who translated gobbets of the Bible, itself an extraordinary paraphrastic artefact. By applying the signifiers of an Aboriginal value-system to their own Judaeo-Christian belief, the missionaries were breaking the language on a wheel. In too many cases their laborious transvestings of the Authorised Version are all that remain of languages now spoken by no one. At a time of fevered research into the origins of Indo-European languages and the gestation of the modern science of linguistics, no attempt was made to codify the wealth of Australian Aboriginal languages. Languages are not simply different sets of labels for the same things; when a language dies, a unique conceptual system which records correspondences and relationships unique to the culture dies with it.

It was not until thirty years ago, when all but thirty or so of the Aboriginal languages were virtually extinct, that white academics began systematically to study them. There being few Aborigines fluent enough in the old languages to contest their authority, they were free to speculate on the relationships between one language or language-group and another, and to debate whether there was ever a single Australian root-language, what might be a language and what a dialect. Experts rose and fell with their theories as the physical expression of Aboriginal thought became a field for contestation and competition between whitefellas, much as Aboriginal art has done.

Aboriginal peoples now find themselves divided on the issue of language; some want a tribal language to be taught as a first language, others English, with one of the tribal languages as a second language, and others Kriol. There are three main varieties of Kriol, one spoken in the Kimberley, another in the Northern Territory and another in the Torres Strait Islands. To complicate matters further, Aboriginal English is seen by some as distinct from both Kriol and standard English and worthy of being systematically taught – but to whom? The burden of acquiring these extra languages, old language to speak to law or ceremonial matters, Kriol or Aboriginal English to speak with young people, and formal English for court cases, land claims and political activity, falls exclusively upon the Aborigines. Kriol is an expression of the blackfellas' desire to communicate; it is high time that whitefellas made the minimal effort that it would require them to learn it, and reciprocated what was in part an act of love. Multilingualism is just one Aboriginal trait that the whitefella would do well to acquire.

When Walter Smith recounted his life experiences to Dick Kimber in 1985 for his memoir, *The Man from Arltunga,* he spoke in Aboriginal English which Kimber renders as exactly as he can. To convert it to formal English would be to weight it down, destroying its momentum. This is Walter's account of the finding of a pair of grinding stones in the Simpson Desert.

> "Alright," old Sandhill Bob said, "we walk that way today. See if we can see him one sandhill, that one. Big sandhill there somewhere. We gottem soakage alright."
>
> He was a good old bushman. He went right where he wanted to go. I followed him.
>
> "There that sandhill!" he said.
>
> Oh, had to go to this big sandhill. He made a big corroboree – made a fire and a corroboree. I was wondering, "I wonder what the old devil's up to now?" Yes, singing away, he was. I was walking around looking for those stones they used to make ntanga, that grass-seed damper. We could see a lot of those bushes growing, with little seeds, brown seeds. I looked around for these stones, I

found one round one, the atuta grinding stone, that's that round stone used to make damper.

I said to him then, "Heh, old man, I got one of that atuta here."

"Oh yes," he said, "where did he come from?"

"Oh, goodness knows," I said, "might be Alice Springs country."

He had a look.

"No," he said, "that stone no coming from Alice Springs. He come from Jervois, this one."

Yes, that stone had come from Jervois. He knew.

He sent me out looking again. He said,

"Getting late, my boy. But you can go back and have a look. See if we findem that athirra."

See, find the dish, the big grind-stone. Athirra. Generally got a little hollow worn in the centre of it, like it's been worn out, you know.

Alright. He's singing away there. That was some old corroboree he knew. I went back. I looked around everywhere. I found a little athirra. It was stuck up in a tree, an old box tree was there. Gawd, it's a stone alright. Brought it down and had a look at it. Yes, athirra. I wondered where this damn thing came from. Took it back to him.

"Here's that athirra, mate, only a little one," I said to him.

He finished his corroboree and put a mark on the ground.

"Oh," he said, "that's the one. I like to see it."

This, unassuming and all as it is, is a great piece of narration. Walter Smith's speech patterns, which are as they are because of his knowledge of the languages of the Eastern Arrernte, result in great flexibility, painting the scene as if by flicks of primary verbiage. A surprising amount of information about the making of ntanga is effortlessly conveyed; there is no attempt to glamorise the setting, among the seed-bearing bushes, with Sandhill Bob, an initiated man, accompanying Smith's search with a long song of country. There is very little of this kind of thing in the body of Australian literature and we could do with more.

There is a problem inherent in the word "Aboriginal" that will not go away. Aborigines are found in all geographic regions, not only Australia. The Canadians have identified a large proportion of their aboriginal population as the Inuit nation, and the New Zealanders all of theirs as a Maori nation, but Australians have not yet found an acceptable name for the emerging Aboriginal nation. We ought perhaps to wait for black Australians to decide what name denotes them all, conscious that this presents them with a problem of convergence for what has always been distinct, and submergence of elements that were once important. Some such phrase as "The Aboriginal Republic of Australia" would be a linguistic nonsense, which doesn't mean that it couldn't be adopted, because the notion of an "aborigine" is already a coinage. There will be a better form of words, if the Aborigines would help us find it.

VII

WHAT ARE WE LIKE?

The majority of non-Aboriginal Australians no longer think of themselves as Europeans, British denizens of an outpost of empire. Even when they did, "British" Australians of Irish blood could hardly have forgotten their ancestors' revulsion at imposed Britishness. Imposed Britishness divided the Australian people along sectarian and class lines, not only alienated the Catholic descendants of Irish Republicans, but sanctioned their persecution by Protestants. Australians should all know Tom Collins's wonderful tirade in *Such is Life* against the importation of British sectarianism to Australia:

> When Australia was first colonised, any sensible man might have foreboded sorrel, cockspur, Scotch thistle &c

> as unwelcome, but unavoidable, adjuncts of settlement. A many-wintered sage might have predicted that some colonist in a fit of criminal folly, would scourge the country with a legacy of foxes, rabbits, sparrow, &c. But a second and clearer-sighted Jeremiah could never have prophesied the deliberate introduction of hydrophobia for dogs, glanders for horses, or Orangeism for men. Yet the latter enterprise has been carried out – whether by John Smith or John Beelzebub, by the Rev. Jones or the Rev. Belphegor, it matters not now. Some one has carried his congenial virus half-way round the globe and tainted a young nation ... [and so on for five pages]

As a child on the way home from a Catholic school in the 1940s, I was often pursued by state-school children, who would block my way singing anti-Catholic songs, daring me to try and push past. Once they had me hemmed in for so long that I wet my pants, which gave them even more ammunition to use against me. Perhaps partly because of my own membership of a hated minority, when Displaced Persons began to arrive in Australia after World War II, I made common cause with them. I learnt German and Italian, and insisted on speaking either one or the other to any "New Australian" who looked as if he or she might understand. I knew what true-blue Australians thought of such dirty foreigners because I heard it at home. What I didn't know was how all non-British immigrant groups had been discriminated against in the historic past, or that DPs were routinely placed in "reception camps", that is, detention centres from which they could only escape by agreeing to work as bonded labour on projects such as the Leigh Creek coalmines, the Tasmanian hydro-electric scheme and the Snowy River project. From the success of these experiments was born the deliberate policy of "multiculturalism" in employment, which means selecting the smallest possible number of people each from the widest available array of nationalities. The new arrivals then have no choice but to learn English, the bosses' language, and to communicate with their fellow-workers in that language. The pattern is repeated in mining operations in the Pilbara and Arnhem Land, in the motor industry and the steel industry, and in the Ord River and Murrumbidgee Irrigation areas. Nabalco is proud to employ thirty nationalities in the bauxite plant at Gove. There is a legend in the motor industry that workers on the assembly line were deliberately placed next to workers with whom they had no language in common, in order to prevent the development of any kind of worker solidarity. Such even-handedness ensured the continuing dominance of the diminishing Anglo-Celt majority, and removed any possibility of the rise of any faction capable of significant insurrection. To the post-war influx of Poles, Latvians, Estonians, Lithuanians, and the Hungarians who joined them after the Revolution, have been added Bosnians, Brazilians, Cambodians, Croats, Cubans, East Timorese, Egyptians, Eritreans, Ethiopians, Filipinos, Haitians, Hmong, Iraqis, Koreans, Kosovars, Kurds, Laotians, Macedonians, Mexicans, Nigerians, Oromos, Punjabis, Samoans, Serbs, Slovenians, Somalis, South Africans, Sudanese, Thais, Tigrayans, Tongans, Turks, Vietnamese and more. With so many contrasting lifestyles, there is only one that can dominate in representation and that is the proto-American, secular, acquisitive, hedonistic insouciance of the you-beaut country. The only culture with sufficient depth and reach to counter such heedless complacency is Aboriginality.

In its pursuit of fantasy whiteness, expressed in the promulgation of the White Australia Policy in 1901, Australian mainstream culture agreed to obscure the historic contribution made to the country's development by Punjabis, "Afghans" and Chinese. More than a hundred ship-loads of Chinese came to New South Wales in 1853–5 to the goldfields on the Turon. When the gold petered out they turned their hands to general trading, market gardening and labouring on projects. They were as abstemious as the Celts were drunken; their prosperity, which resulted from years of hard work and harder rations, was held against them. Many of their settlements have been deliberately obliterated in an effort to write them out of the history of Australia's development. It is only because of the intercession of my great-uncle, Sir John Jensen, that Chinese joss-houses in Bendigo were not knocked down in 1939 at the time of the expansion of the munitions factory. To this day Chinese come to the goldfields cemeteries to seek out the graves of their ancestral kin and pay their respects, while the vast majority of the graves of the Anglo-Celt diggers remain unmarked hummocks, often torn up and obliterated by scrub regrowth or European weeds, visited by no one.

The so-called Afghans who were recruited in the 1860s to operate the camel trains that were for many years the only lines of supply in central Australia came from countries as far apart as Baluchistan, Egypt, Kashmir, Persia, the Punjab, Rajasthan, Sind and Turkey and lived in separate sections of the towns they helped to build. Those who married tended to marry Aboriginal women and, unlike the "British", were happy to acknowledge the children they had with Aboriginal women as their own. The success of the

"Afghans" in traversing the desert is partly due to the fact that, unlike Burke and Wills, they let the Aborigines teach them how to live off the land. The cameleers made chapatis from grass-seed meal ground on the Aborigines' grinding stones, and flavoured their wild meat stews with Australian aromatics. If it had been down to them Australians would now be eating kangaroo-meat instead of beef, and Aborigines and others would be able still to live on bush tucker.

Multiculturalism is now understood as a superior alternative to assimilationism. What this means is that ethnic and cultural minorities may express their difference without fear of discrimination; they can follow their own religion, provided they have the money to build and staff religious establishments, eat their own food, celebrate their national feasts with picnics in public parks and publish newspapers in their own language. Mainstream Australian media, however, are monoglot; only SBS shows news broadcasts in foreign languages, none of which addresses matters of immediate concern to ethnic minorities trying to come to terms with Australia. Italian news is an overseas service of the RAI. News in Spanish comes not from the Philippines or Mexico but from Spain. Rather than helping Italian Australians or Spanish-speaking Australians to deal with the issues that arise from their experience of life in Australia, SBS simply informs Italian- and Spanish-speakers in Australia about events in Europe.

All Australia's ethnic minorities are expected to concur in the view that Australia is the best country in the world. The difference between Aboriginal peoples and other minorities is that for them Australia, and a specific part of Australia at that, is the *only* country in the world. They did not choose it and they cannot escape it, for outside their country their existence is chaotic and meaningless. To accept Australia's Aboriginality is not to reject "multiculturalism" by imposing a single culture on all Australians, because Aboriginality includes a multitude of cultures and languages and is itself a blueprint for genuine multiculturalism, in which everyone speaks more than one language and there is no imposed lingua franca. Aboriginal society requires individuals to marry across language groups; users of the same country are required to perform corroboree and ceremonial together in whichever language is appropriate to the occasion, but not to surrender their separateness or the contrasting aspects of their culture. Groups who do not practise circumcision, for example, are not derided and persecuted by groups who do, or vice versa. Aboriginality provides a better template for twenty-first-century Australia than a phoney multiculturalism that serves only to increase the dominance of a proto-British elite, which insists on wriggling up to the US and replicating the least impressive aspects of British policy.

The common perception from within the country is that white Australians and black Australians are very different. Outsiders are rarely in a position to assess the family resemblance between the two groups, but I for one am struck by the degree of influence exerted by Aboriginal people on the formation of the Australian character and way of life. Australians, despite the official policy of multiculturalism, aren't genuinely cosmopolitan, but they aren't British either. They exhibit neither British manners nor British values. If Australians should doubt this, they have only to travel to England, where they will feel less at home than they would in any other part of the world. Their gestures are too ample, their voices too loud, their approach too direct and their spontaneity embarrassing. Their lack of class consciousness mystifies the English who are obsessed by calculations of relative status, and inordinately anxious to avoid the kind of gaffe that would betray inferiority. Australians are amused by the number of times English people will say "please", "thank you" and "excuse me", unaware perhaps that in such a crowded country it is important to avoid friction. Aborigines are not given to "please" and "thank you" either, when "gibbit" will do. Even Australians who gradually learn to mute their responses and respect the Englishman's desperate need to believe that he is alone in the midst of a crowd will not succeed in passing as British; after thirty years' residence in the country, I am still startled by taxi-drivers and their ilk asking me how long I've been over there and when I am going home. People who should know better ask me whether I think the way I do because I come from barbarous and backward Australia. And I probably do, but I'm damned if I'll give them the pleasure of hearing me say it.

Australians cannot be confused with any other Commonwealth peoples; they behave differently from Canadians, South Africans and even New Zealanders. It is my contention, diffidently offered, that the Australian national character derives from the influence of the Aborigines whose dogged resistance to an imported and inappropriate culture has affected our culture more deeply than is usually recognised. From the beginning of colonisation, the authorities' deepest fear was that settlers would degenerate and go native. In many subtle and largely unexplored ways they did just that. Indeed, they may already partake in more Aboriginality than they know, in the way they speak and what they say and leave unsaid.

Australian egalitarianism is usually perceived to be the result of the harsh circumstances which drove settlers to make the long journey half-way round the world and the fact that the free settler had scant reason to consider himself a cut above the emancipated convict, especially when so little stood between him and a conviction for poddy-dodging, cattle rustling or simply not having the necessary paperwork. The influence of the Aborigines in deflating whitefellas' pretensions to gentility has nowhere been considered. Australians still place great store on an individual's ability to do what he is asking others to do, whether in terms of endurance or skill or courage, and that too may be a part of their Aboriginal inheritance. You will not find it in Britain, where rank and class still count for more than any personal talent or skill.

Joseph Furphy, writing as Tom Collins in *Such is Life*, remarks, as he ponders the influx of farmers driven out of the Riverina by drought in 1883:

> There was no end of them. Week after week, month after month, they came stringing-in from seven-syllabled localities on all points of the compass; some with sunburnt wives and graduated sets of supple-jointed, keen-sighted children – the latter, I grieve to admit, distinctly affirming

> that disquieting theory which assumes evolution of immigrating races toward the aboriginal type.

The point about Tom Collins is that he is wrong about everything. Yet migrants to anywhere do come to resemble the aboriginal population of that anywhere not by "evolution" but as they are influenced by the Aborigines' proximity. To be sure migrants to Australia interbred with Aborigines, but they ostracised their offspring so that they would not be seen to be turning brown. Unless we assume that Collins's sunburnt wives were Aboriginal, which given Collins's obtuseness they may have been, he is referring to full-blood white children who are apparently turning Aboriginal. Collins ascribes their greater agility and keener vision to growing Aboriginality. If they were good at tracking, if they were exceptionally observant, it would have been because the Aborigines who performed menial tasks on the Riverina farms spent time with them and taught them how to see, how to read the language of the bush. If they rode like blackfellas, it was because blackfellas taught them to ride. Since Tom Collins observed it, the Aboriginalisation of our children has continued by means of heaven only knows what unseen agency. Untold numbers of Australian parents have become aware that their children have turned "feral", that they have no ambition, covet no man's goods, and are happy to follow wherever the waves are, living by and for the moment, and occasionally attending secret gatherings deep in national forests where strange things are done and said and strange substances ingested.

The evasiveness of white Australians is another sign of Aboriginal influence. Australians find the notion of a single fixed identity which must be known to all at all times deeply disturbing. The British may have refused to carry ID cards and will occasionally say "no names, no pack-drill", meaning that no awkward questions will be asked, but generally speaking English "reserve" is a myth. In Britain accent places everyone in a neat pigeonhole of class and affluence; social intercourse is largely a process of identifying and locating individuals in a dense social context, which in turn produces a diffidence very different from Australian evasiveness. Under the constant pressure from American cultural imperialism Australians are becoming more loquacious; my father's generation would have regarded the endlessly babbling characters of Australian TV soaps with instinctive revulsion. In life as distinct from TV Australian shyness is real; it is based on a principle of waiting to see whether an individual is worthy, "a good bloke", "dinkum" etc., rather than figuring out how much money he's got and whom he might be related to as a ground for friendship. Australians don't, as Americans do, confront total strangers with a barrage of questions, "Where'y'from?" etc., and when so confronted tend to give non-committal responses, rather than spill their guts. The preferred approach is easy, rather than confrontational.

Similarly the Aboriginal way is not to confront or interrogate anyone, whether a first acquaintance or an old friend. Blackfellas never put themselves in a position where they are asking to be lied to; what you want to tell you tell, and what you are silent about remains unspoken. The reticence that is intrinsic to Aboriginal relationships is also a governing principle in the Australian concept of mateship. Traditionally mates don't pry into each other's affairs. Mates give each other space, allow each other to come and go, and to retain a measure of privacy, especially about their past and about intimate relationships. Whatever name they choose to give is good enough. As Mitchell says in Lawson's story "The Man Who Forgot", "... as for a name, that's nothing. I don't know mine, and I've had eight."

Though self-revelation is unwelcome and uninvited by Australians of all hues, yarning is a social duty. Australians used to take trouble to spin a good yarn; the best are those (like *Clancy of the Overflow* or *The Loaded Dog*) in which some incident in real life is expertly spun into something almost mythical. Another Lawson story, "Stragglers", published in 1896, describes the tradition:

> There are tally-lies; and lies about getting tucker by trickery; and long-tramp-with-heavy-swag-and-no-water lies; and lies about getting the best of squatters and bosses-over-the-board; and droving, fighting, racing, gambling and drinking lies. Lies *ad libitum*; and every true Australian bushman must try his best to tell a bigger out-back lie than the last bush-liar.

I once heard Tid Dignam, father of the actor Arthur Dignam, describe a game of ping-pong in such dramatic detail that it became a mini-Trojan War. It took me some years to register that Tid was part-Aboriginal and that the making of memorable stories was part of Aboriginal culture many aeons before whitefellas started doing it round the boree log. In Tid the connection between the Australian and the Aboriginal was seamless and therefore unseen.

For Australians nomenclature remains almost absurdly problematic, and this too is an aspect of the Aboriginal inheritance. Aborigines had several names, some to be used by the same skin and others for kin related in different ways, and perhaps another for outsiders. This was reflected in Australian whitefella behaviour, especially during the Depression. A newcomer on the track would be given a version of his name for use by his new mates; only such nicknames were ever used, in case the authorities came looking for wife-starvers or absconders. Prying into such matters was not encouraged. The men protected each other by a studious ignorance, a technique they might have picked up from the Aborigines. The Aborigines too wore their whitefella names as aliases, preferring to be identified to strangers by the station they were attached to and their nickname, rather than their skin names which were already known to all who needed to know them.

Observers of white Australian life are struck by the degree of segregation between the sexes, which cannot be explained by the prevailing mores of the countries they came from either at the time or now. Aboriginal society too is deeply segregated; men and women are used to spending long periods in the company of their own sex. The more important the occasion and the larger the gathering, the more likely it is that women will gather in one area and men in another, just as white Australian men gather round the beer keg, leaving the women to talk among themselves. One explanation of the Australian mania for sport of all kinds is that sport is the only remaining area of human activity that is still rigorously segregated. Sport, the most important element in Australian cultural life, is one area where Aboriginal people have been able to claim the respect that is their due. It is possibly the least problematic area when it comes to claiming Aboriginality for Australia. The New Zealanders didn't shrink from calling their national rugby team the All-Blacks, though they weren't; Australians have preferred to call theirs after animals rather than people.

Non-Aboriginal Australians no longer understand Kriol but if they imagine that Aboriginality has left no mark upon their language they are wrong. Not only is Australian English studded with Aboriginal words, the unmistakeable intonation and accent bear the imprint of Aboriginality. The Anglo-Celt settlers came speaking an array of Scotch and Irish brogues, as well as the burrs of provincial England. The Australian accent bears scant resemblance to any of these. Canadian English is more Scots and Irish than Australian English. Linguists seeking to explain the divergence of Australian English have connected it to cockney thieves' cant, and some such descent may be assumed, perhaps, though Australian English contains no equivalent of the cockney glottals, in which the sound is made further back in the throat, so that "chocolate" becomes, for example, "chocklick". When I first heard blackfellas speak I stupidly thought that they were imitating the way white-fellas speak, which just goes to show how upside-down gubbas' assumptions can be. The transfer must have happened the other way about; the broad flat vowels, complex diphthongs and murmuring nasalities of spoken Australian English must have come to us from Aboriginal languages. It stands to reason that men who spent their waking hours in the company of black farmhands would have begun to mimic the consonants and vowels of Kriol, if only to make themselves more readily understood. Children who were brought up by black women among black children would also have picked up the sounds they heard around them.

In the way we behave, the way we speak, the way we feel about lots of things, white Australians exhibit the effects of the gentle but insistent and pervasive influence of black Australia, passed down through our culture as surely as white genes passed into the black genome. The more we try to deny it, the more the inextricability of black and white will become obvious, if not to Australians themselves then certainly to outsiders. This is our badge of hope; we should wear it with pride.

VIII

IF NOT TERRA NULLIUS, THEN WHAT?

The achievement of post-colonial status involves more than simply changing the words "British Subject" on Australian passports to "Australian citizen", for one expression is not a contradiction of the other. So far we are all British subjects as well as Australian citizens, and apparently anxious to stay that way, given the 1999 vote against becoming a republic. Post-colonial status will not be ours to claim until Australians have defined, fought for and achieved self-determination. Until we do that we will remain in the toils of the identity crisis that results in solemn absurdities like Australia Day, a holiday of obligation that has no counterpart in less insecure societies. Australia Day is celebrated on 26 January, the day of the year on which Governor Phillip "took formal possession" of the part of the continent that would be called "New South Wales", a ridiculously inappropriate name that still survives. In the mangled English typical of a semi-literate colony, 26 January is described by the Australia Day Council as the "biggest day of celebration in the country" (rather than the day of greatest celebration) and "the day for everyone who calls themselves Australian" (rather than all who call themselves Australian). If you call yourself Australian, then you are Australian, or so it would seem.

In the 2001 census, 410,003 Australians claimed Aboriginal and Torres Strait Islander origin, a huge increase on the 1991 total of 265,371. The explanation is to be found not in a population explosion among Aboriginal communities but in a change in the perception of Aboriginal identity itself. Moreover, as in those ten years more and more Australians had been investigating their family history, hitherto unacknowledged Aboriginal forebears had been rediscovered. More people are now aware of their Aboriginal inheritance and desirous of claiming it. Many people who came out as "black" in 2001 had never lived as Aborigines and had never had to endure the discrimination and abuse that Aborigines coped with daily, but no Aborigine inveighed against their claim to Aboriginality. A similar situation occurred in the United States in the 1920s and '30s: native American groups given head-rights to income from oil extraction in their homelands were astonished to see how many of their whitefella neighbours claimed membership of the tribes and signed on for head-rights, having successfully concealed their tribal ancestry (if any) till that time. There are now more Aboriginal people in Australia than at any previous time in the continent's history. Aboriginality is growing and building a momentum which could catch up more and more of us, bearing us towards an interesting and very special future.

The recognition that Australia was not an empty land when European settlement began has resulted in a good deal of pointless and acrimonious argument about notions of ownership. Aborigines do not consider themselves proprietors of territory, it is argued, therefore they should not be given proprietorial rights, which include the right to sell land as a commodity. Squatters did claim proprietorial rights, sometimes over tracts of land that were so vast that the idea was meaningless. The cattle-king Sidney Kidman bought Thule Station in 1887, Cowarie in 1895, Owen Springs in 1896, followed by Alton Downs, Annandale, Caryapundy, Clayton, Haddon Downs, Mount Nor'West, Pandi Pandi, Roseberth, Tickalara, Eringa and Austral Downs, as well as part shares in other stations. Though vast numbers of cattle died in the drought of 1900–03, Kidman, who had other strings to his bow, was not wiped out. Once again he was able to profit by the misfortunes of others. He bought Carandotta and Lake Albert and sold them on six months later at a profit. He then bought Bullo Downs, Sandringham, Glengyle, Peake Downs, Innamincka and Mundowdna. He was now sole leaseholder of an area greater than that of Great Britain, Ireland included. If Kidman had a home it was his wife's birthplace of Kapunda, where he built a large house for himself and his family, but he had no intention of living his life out there. He eventually moved his business to Adelaide and donated the house to the Education Department to serve as a high school. Although Kidman owned land, or Crown leases to land, there is no sign in this career of astonishing acquisitiveness that he cared two hoots for any of it, still less that he felt he belonged to it. In this respect Kidman is like the rest of his ilk, who acquired huge tracts of land only to lose them or sell them. They were prepared to fight the original inhabitants for the right to exclude them from the land that was their life, but they never became attached to the land they fought for. Just as they had trifled with black women, they trifled with the land, held it for a time and dumped it.

Few of the adventurers who "opened up" the Australian

hinterland managed to found a dynasty. In the words of Mary Durack:

> Many of the descendants of the old "first families" [of Western Australia] still figure prominently in local public and business life, their origins never forgotten even though their original properties have for the most part changed hands many times. The idea of hereditary landholdings died hard, if it died at all, but continued ownership was subject not only to the exigencies of drought and depression but to the lure of new pastures and more lucrative prospects in conditions of developing settlement. In fact Australian families who have retained their original estates beyond the second or third generation are few and far between.

Unless of course you count the Aborigines.

The evidence from the Durack family itself suggests that the driving force behind the opening up of virgin land was less a desire to found a dynasty than to acquire money and power in as short a time as possible. Patrick Durack first took up a cocky-run near Goulburn in 1855; in 1868 he moved out towards Cooper's Creek and the Diamantina, where he and his brother-in-law John Costello took up land on spec in various names until their total holding was calculated at 35,000 square miles. The aim was to take up virgin country, stock it, improve it and sell it on at a profit, and this Durack and Costello did over and over again. In 1879 their land hunger drove a posse of Durack men westwards toward the Kimberley, where once more they helped themselves to the "pick of the Ord and Fitzroy country". A sub-theme in Mary Durack's *Kings in Grass Castles* is the resistance of the Durack women, their desire to live where their dead were buried, the beginnings of their attachment to place – their Aboriginalisation perhaps. The Durack properties on Cooper's Creek were among the first lost in the crash of 1890, largely as a consequence of the Duracks' own speculations in land. Such openers-up of country neither stay long enough nor wait long enough in the country to see how it works before setting about disrupting it, killing or driving off its native inhabitants, building roads, making boundaries. The Duracks understood so little of what they were doing in the Kimberley that they couldn't even position their original dwelling at Argyle high enough to escape the rising waters of the Behn River in the wet season. They were surrounded by blacks but they didn't ask them. It doesn't take much bushcraft to find evidence of periodic flood; evidently they didn't even look. Yet they dared to dream of a massive interference in a river system that they understood so poorly that their first expedition was a disaster and they were repeatedly lost on the second. Patrick Durack is credited with the original conception of the grand scheme of using the Ord River for irrigation, considered by many to have been an expensive disaster.

Not for nothing are these users of vast tracts of the Australian hinterland known as squatters. In the topsy-turvy Antipodean way, a word that denotes an abuser of the rights of others has come to signify "old money", an upper class, resulting in the coinage "squattocracy". The land they took up was actually leased from the Crown; what they bought and sold was not land but leases. Today, the vast majority of Australians are not squatters but "owner-occupiers" who have acquired the freehold of tiny parcels of land, quarter-acre lots for the most part. Freehold ought to represent a historic title established many generations before, with a paper trail of charters and deeds that confirms its legitimacy. In Australia Crown land has been declared freehold by governmental fiat. Usually in return for a money payment, but sometimes by a mere "stroke of the pen", lands leased by the Crown have been re-gazetted as the inalienable property of individuals. One day some clever lawyer will question the legality of all such arbitrary creations of title; so far they remain unchallenged.

Land held by lease is not the property of the occupier to do with as he pleases. Rather, it is held in trust for future generations and the leaseholder can be held liable for dilapidation and degradation that occur during his stewardship. Freehold carries no such limitation or liability, because the only person who stands to lose by mismanagement is the owner, until, that is, a body of law sufficient to deal with the environmental impact of land clearance, swimming-pool building, air-conditioning installation, waste disposal and so forth is developed. The Crown is the most absentee of absentee landlords; no protest is ever heard from the Crown Estates Office against the arbitrary creation and granting of freeholds and no action has ever been taken against a leaseholder for abuse of the land. Arguably every holder of a Crown leasehold should be liable for reckless clearing of the land for stock, planting of exotic feed grasses that had annihilated native grasses, and the depredations of his hard-hoofed animals, and for salination and the degradation of surface water, but there is not enough money in the entire industry to pay what restoration would cost. If Aboriginalisation was achieved, the absentee landlord, the British Crown, would be replaced by an in-dwelling entity, the Aboriginal people (i.e. all the people) of Australia.

If Australia were to be recognised as an Aboriginal nation, Crown leasehold would vanish as a concept in Australian law because the Crown's claim to the land would be seen as invalid or extinct. What was held in trust for the Crown would then be held in trust for the nation, the new Aboriginal nation; effectively land would be nationalised. Lawyers, having succeeded in bringing even trial by jury into disrepute, are capable of buggering up any good idea, especially if it looks like conflicting with their ability to make a fat living out of the misfortunes of others, and they will do their best to make the nationalisation of land a disaster. Handled correctly, it could produce a situation in which claims by particular Aboriginal groups and individuals were seen to be claims for specific uses rather than ownership, except in those cases where the historic equivalent of a freehold title held by an identifiable individual could be proved, as in the famous precedent of Eddie Mabo. This would have the fully intended consequence of rendering obsolete the ramified and contradictory case law of Aboriginal title which has resulted in the escalation of costs in land claims cases to the point where white lawyers are creaming off more than the market value of the land in question and beggaring their Aboriginal clients. Existing freeholds could be ratified, except in exceptional cases where a pre-existing right of use or occupancy was recognised. If land were to become a national resource, governments could exercise closer control of its exploitation, and citizens would have a clearer perception that restrictions on land-use, for example, were made in their interest and ought to be observed by everyone. Ideally action would be taken to rehabilitate land ruined by inappropriate use, but as the most destructive schemes have also been the most expensive and the least profitable, it is not easy to see where the money would come from.

The leaseholders of the major part of Australian land historically speculated, devastated, and disappeared. The traveller across inland Australia will move from abandoned homestead to abandoned homestead, along lines of collapsed fences, past heaps of machinery rusting into the ground, to abandoned townships that once had churches and law courts, concert halls and racetracks, and are now no more than truck stops. If you travel northwards from Port Augusta past Quorn and Hawker, you don't find yourself travelling into a prosperous hinterland; even though the road runs in tandem with a railway, there is very little development until you find yourself in the midst of the gouged black landscape that is the Leigh Creek coalmine; a few kilometres to the north, the Strzelecki Track follows an old Aboriginal thoroughfare towards Innamincka, where cattle-king Kidman built his fortunes on 11,000 square miles. To the east the homesteads of Kudriemitchie and Coongie lie abandoned. A few kilometres further on you will find the ruins of the ambitious town of Farina, designed to be the centre of a wheat belt that never materialised. During the 1870s, after a run of good seasons, a tide of settlers moved northwards into the Willochra Plains, taking up one-mile selections for wheat farming. In their wake sprang up towns like Eurelia, Hammond, Johnburgh, Carrieton, Gordon, Cradock, Wilson, all now virtually deserted. The railway, originally intended to carry the grain harvests from Farina to Port Augusta ends at Marree, where the traveller must decide to go either to the east of Lake Eyre along the empty Birdsville track, or to the west past the ruined homesteads of Wanganna, William Creek, Box Creek, Edwards Creek, Warrina and Mount Dutton to Oodnadatta. Oodnadatta and Marree, like Windorah, Birdsville and Betoota, Tibooburra and Milparinka, are more like trading posts than towns, consisting of no more than police station and lock-up, pub, general store, truck stop and fuel distributor. Innamincka township was abandoned in 1952, leaving as its sole monument a pile of bottles four or five feet high and 200 yards long. Now even the bottle heap has disappeared.

When sheep replaced wheat in the arid inland, another kind of pest swarmed, proliferated, devastated and withdrew. At Mount Gipps the biggest shearing shed in Australia, 150 feet long and 75 feet wide, built in the 1870s out of local stone, together with all the buildings that once clustered round it, has disappeared. None of the whitefellas who once made a living in such places as stockmen, tank-sinkers, hawkers, shearers, policemen, hoteliers or bullockies, felt sufficient attachment to the country to stay there through drought and flood, or even to return when times got better. If the country couldn't earn its keep, the white man wanted none of it. And even when he could make a profit, the white man tended to take his money and run. Only the Aborigines stayed.

Of all the transitory devastators of country, miners must be the worst. They arrived like locusts, stripping every vestige of vegetation off the ground that they believed to be hiding their lode, riddling it with holes and tunnels and pimpling it with mullock heaps, reducing it to mud and dust at best, and poisonous slime dumps at worst. Behind them came those who preyed on them, tax-collectors, publicans, prostitutes. Within weeks towns sprang up where their winnings could be sucked away in return for alcohol. The story of boom and bust in Australia has been told many times, and hardly bears repeating here. Nowadays mining is not a matter of fossickers and battlers staking individual claims but of corporations investing in massively industrialised open-cut mining. The ore is carted away along temporary railway tracks laid across the desert. The miners live in trailer camps that will move when they do. Occasionally, as at Jabiru and Gove, the company will build a dormitory suburb where off-duty workers can enjoy "a sophisticated recreational lifestyle", but these too will be left to rot into the ground when the company pulls out. Oil doesn't need people to extract the riches from the ground; when the drilling teams install their donkey well and lay their pipeline, they too up stakes and vanish, and the retailers who sold them fast food and alcohol disappear with them. Even the most important provincial towns, even the likes of Broken Hill, where billions of dollars worth of precious metals have been extracted from the ground, are withering. Their huge hotels are cavernous and empty; of the shops along the main streets, a few sell fast food, a few more are opportunity shops of one kind or another, and even more are empty, their windows papered or painted over. The flight from the inland continues; these days not even a new gold rush would get the people back again. The nearest they'd get to the diggings would be to invest in a few mining company shares.

Whole mountains are shipped away from the Pilbara each year, and not because selling off the finest-grade iron ore in the world makes us rich. There is no highest bidder for iron ore; we sell it off to anyone who will have it at any price they will pay. Whole landscapes from horizon to horizon have been ripped open for coal; entire Australian forests are chipped into building boards and paper. As I write these words, the news has come that despite $20m worth of dredging the mouth of the Murray is once more choked with sand and there is no point in removing it, because if we dredged continuously the flow from the greatest river system in the continent would still be insufficient to keep the sandbar from building up. If we truly felt that this country was our home we could not despoil it in this manner; we are trashing it because we suspect that it belongs to someone else. Every now and then someone comes up with a scheme like Bob Hawke's One Billion Trees Programme of 1989. It was meant to begin the replacement of the estimated 15–16 billion trees removed by clearing, but the wrong trees were planted the wrong way, the follow-through funding wasn't in place and the labour wasn't available. Even the trees planted by Hawke himself died, and were replaced, not once but several times. In any case, it is even more urgent to slow down the rate of clearing than it is to try to revegetate cleared areas where the climatic conditions are now unsuitable for the re-establishment of the original plant populations (supposing Hawke and his myrmidons had got them right). The challenge of land restoration that faces Australia requires, not pocket-money, volunteer labour, sporadic goodwill and brief bursts of misdirected activity, but a major investment of time, money and expertise in a co-ordinated campaign that would be harder to organise and even more expensive to wage than any war in history.

Australians now travel further throughout Australia than ever they did before, as tourists; in recreational vehicles of all kinds they penetrate into the remotest areas, driving thousands of kilometres to see funny-shaped rocks, taking photographs of the rocks and themselves with the rocks, to show the people back home. They are on safari in their own land, treating their birthplace as if it were an exotic, thrillingly foreign wilderness, travelling from well-appointed campsite or hotel to another campsite or hotel, an evening here and evening there on the best beaten of tracks. The people who stay longest in these remote places, and take jobs servicing the itinerant Australian tourist in

Australia, are not indigenous, or native Australians, or even residents, but British backpackers.

If we climbed out of the recreational vehicle and sat on the ground we might begin to get the message that we can't afford to hear, the message that since contact Aborigines have never stopped transmitting. The land is the source of everything; if we rip it up and sell it off we will perish with it, or else move on in our restless European way to devastate someone else's country – or planet.

Aboriginality is not simply a cluster of behaviours and characteristics that individuals could claim for themselves and recognise in themselves; it is more importantly a characteristic of the continent itself. Australia will be truly self-governing and independent only when it has recognised its inherent and ineradicable Aboriginality. The island continent was marked and managed by its people for 50,000 years or so. We are only just beginning to recognise how the continuous presence of Aborigines shaped the continent and preserved its fragile ecosystems. It is already too late perhaps for us to learn how to reverse the devastation inflicted by whitefellas in the short space of 200 years, but some attempt at damage limitation must be made. Recognising the custodianship of the land as a sacred trust would not be a bad place to start.

IX

OUR PLACE

Supposing Australians accepted their destiny and, as if by an act of transubstantiation, declared their country and themselves Aboriginal, down would come the Blue Ensign with the Southern Cross and up would go the emblem of the black sky, the red earth and the golden sun. What happened after that would rather depend upon the will of the people. To accept Aboriginality would be to deny the validity of the annexation of the continent for the British monarch. The planting of Union Jacks on tiny bits of it would be seen from the Aboriginal point of view and understood to have been entirely insignificant. The concomitant of accepting Aboriginality, then, is denial of the initial act of colonisation. In this version of events colonisation was attempted and failed.

It has never been clear to me whether Australia in its present state can properly be described as post-colonial, because there seems to be nothing post- about it. As long as the Crown remained the landlord, it seemed to make little odds that the Privy Council no longer ruled in cases of Australian law, especially as the original inhabitants had rights under the common law which were being eroded by Australian case law. As long as the British head of state was required to ratify Australian parliamentary process it seemed to me that the country was a colony pure and simple. The influence exerted by foreign corporations as the principal exploiters of Australian resources forces Australia into unequal competition with the poorest dependent nations in the world, reinforcing the colonial stereotype. Emerging as an Aboriginal Republic might not materially alter this situation, but it would signify an awareness of the true facts of the case and a willingness to accept them, along with a new role as a chief representative of such nations in the world forum. Instead of falsely identifying with the exploiter, Australia would stand alongside the exploited. This might involve a loss of prestige, but Australians have never had much truck with prestige. Australia's voluntary identification with the largest group in the United Nations, namely the emerging post-colonial republics, could provide an opportunity for genuine leadership, rather than the eternal flunkeydom that is our present lot.

In the past Australia has truckled to the other WASP world powers, done their dirty work for them in the hopes of sharing the rewards, and has been snubbed, hard, and still we have been first to offer our eager services even in a case as dodgy and inexcusable as the massive assault on Iraq. If Australia were to recognise itself as an Aboriginal nation it could with one bound free itself from its spurious identification with the WASP "axis of evil", which would have instant and important consequences for national security, given the inevitability of an increase in international terrorism after the orgy of destruction in Iraq. If we followed the Aboriginal course, we could follow Aboriginal precedent and simply absent ourselves from activities that we knew to be evil and pointless. Riding on the coat-tails of Britain, itself on the coat-tails of the USA, has brought Australia neither power nor wealth, and has cost us moral authority in our rather tenuous sphere of influence. The respect Australia earned in its handling of Timor it lost in the Gulf.

The history of Australia's participation in Britain's wars is a travailed one, in which Australia has given far more than it got. Though we talk easily of a dominant Anglo-Celt culture, it should never be forgotten that this contained within it painful and unresolved conflict which distorted whitefella interaction at every point. The convicts were preponderantly of Irish descent, for the same reasons that if the experiment were tried again in our own time the convicts would be mostly black. The Irish were not only the criminalised class; they filled the lowest ranks of enforcers as well. Only the officer class was actually Anglo. Some of the Irish identified with their oppressors and tried with varying success to curry favour with them; others remembered the traditions of the rapparees and bog-trotters and did their best to fleece and despoil them. Ned Kelly is an Australian hero because, in mythical if not historical terms, he is the quintessential rebel against British suzerainty represented by landholders, police and the judiciary. The official voice of Australia may have been reliably pro-British, but the gut feeling of Australia was always to some extent anti-British, and that extent is growing. The elite in Australia used to ape English manners and spoke a parody of Oxbridge English, but it does so no longer. No native Australian now calls England home, as many did when I was growing up.

The Irish section of the Anglo-Celt hegemony reacted bitterly to the pointless carnage of the First World War. The feeling that Australia should not get involved was still strong when the war drums began beating again in the 1930s. Australians who believed that if they fought alongside the British in Europe and Africa, Britain would defend Australia, were eventually proved wrong when Singapore was allowed to fall virtually undefended. The Commonwealth Air Training Scheme in which all available pilot recruits were trained for the European conflict went ahead, leaving Australia with no air defences. When the Japanese invaded the Northern Territory, Australia had no comeback. Ironically, after the war, Japan, Australia's prime antagonist in the Pacific, was gradually transformed into Australia's most valued trading partner, as Britain dumped Australia and turned its face, if somewhat coquettishly, towards Europe.

Prime Minister Howard took his cue from the resounding defeat of the Republican movement in the referendum of 1999 to exaggerate Australia's fading Britishness by appointing an inoffensive but undistinguished Anglican archbishop as governor-general, with results that are now history. Most Australians had not given the matter of the governor-generalship much thought until the press campaign against the unfortunate Peter Hollingworth; then they asked themselves what a governor-general did for them and the answer was obvious. If Australia were to declare its Aboriginality, all the trappings of fake Britishness could be ditched; the states already have premiers and do not need governors, but if we felt that some such outrigger was needed for the ship of state, we could appoint a council of elders who could comment on legislation from the point of view of Aboriginal law and custom, if they felt like it. Otherwise their function could be, as the gubernatorial function is, largely ceremonial. Already, Aboriginal ceremonial is being built into formal occasions in Australia, though in a rather shy and constrained fashion. If Australia was officially Aboriginal these ceremonies would be more than lip-service and the people participating would have a clearer idea of the meaning of the ceremonial gestures of welcome and sharing. More of us would understand language, and appreciate the nuances of the kind of celebration that was being performed. If New Zealanders can reduce huge football stadiums to a breathless hush by performing the haka, we can dance too.

Republicanism has so far been presented to the Australian public as a negative affair, with no charisma in either the idea or the personnel who presented it. If the project were to create not just a republic but an Aboriginal republic, it would be a lot sexier. Exploring the idea of just how

Aboriginality could be expressed in modern political institutions would be really exciting. Cutting loose discreditable connections is a condition of achieving genuine independence. If America and Britain were our most important trading partners this might cost us, but they aren't. Australia's most important export markets are, as Aboriginal markets were, in Asia. Britain and the USA could hardly do less for Australia than they do already. Assumed or confessed Aboriginality could give us the right to examine the conditions under which foreign corporations hold leases on vast tracts of Australian land and rights to extraction of minerals, and an opportunity to renegotiate or cancel them.

All law depends upon a version of events and the version of Australian history that describes colonisation as a failed enterprise would be a new one. In this version, the colonial authorities tried to criss-cross Australia with roads and railways, tried to populate the country, tried to build up a provincial society, tried to make money out of the country, tried to accumulate the gravitas of a world power, failed repeatedly and finally gave up. The colonists have now retreated to the beach where they originally landed; the inland remains indomitable. During the brief suzerainty of the British, the British legal system operated in Australia at the same time as Aboriginal law and in conflict with it; the consequences are such that Aboriginal law cannot now be reapplied. In any case, no single body of Aboriginal law would ever have applied to the Australian population as a whole, and the default legal system would probably have to be British common law, modified as it has been by Australian case law and precedent. The intricacies of reconciling the two systems are well illustrated by the tortuous and ruinously expensive legal proceedings surrounding native title claims. A unilateral declaration of independence from the Crown that did not involve a simplification of process in these matters would be compromised from the outset. It would be a bitter irony indeed if Australia's recognition of its own Aboriginality were to prove yet another stick to beat the blackfellas with. If we begin with the idea that the country is an Aboriginal country, that title is vested in the Aboriginal people, it should be easier, not harder, for specific groups to establish specific rights outside the bundle of rights held in common. Australians have already begun to respect such rights where they have been established; it should be possible to develop a system where such matters are decided by consultation rather than by litigation.

Once Australia became an Aboriginal country it could join the other post-colonial nations, who are numerically the largest voting community in the UN. We would no longer be seen as a puppy running alongside the US and Britain, but as a leader in our own right. In an operation like the defence of East Timor, we would not be tempted to beg the US for assistance only to be humiliated when it was denied. We could invent our own management styles, if indeed we have not already done so. It was noticeable that the Australians fought a different war in Iraq from that waged by both the British and the Americans – noticeable to Australians, that is, because British and American media seldom mentioned the fact that Australia was involved at all.

As a hunter-gatherer nation, Australia could play a further role in world affairs by making common cause with other hunter-gatherer peoples, all of whom are taking a terrible hammering. Most are isolated from the mainstream, as presently Aborigines are; the emergence on the world stage of a hunter-gatherer nation, with policy aims and initiatives that are consonant with hunter-gatherer values, could be a lifeline for such peoples, and provide useful precedents in their struggle to protect country, heritage and habitat from annihilation. The recognition of hunter-gatherer culture would involve the establishment of networks and institutions where the cultures could be learned in context. For example, Australians are not the only people who practised firestick farming; it would be of assistance to those trying to recreate the prairie ecology of North America to work together with those trying to restore the open grasslands of Australia.

What has been offered here is not a blueprint for the future but the suggestion of a way forward. It is made in the full awareness of the extent of racism in Australia, of the fear and loathing that was harvested by Pauline Hanson, and of the appalling situation that prevails in so many of the Aboriginal homelands. From some points of view, it has never been less likely that Australians would recognise their own Aboriginality, but the way to light is through darkness, and this darkest hour could be just before our dawn as a genuinely new nation. Some of the groundwork is already in place. We have a choice of building on it, and precious little option otherwise. Australians have never lacked courage or originality. Add imagination to the mix, and there will be no stopping us. Daring to think the unthinkable is a necessary prelude to doing the impossible. Disagree with me by all means, dear reader, but don't dismiss me out of hand. Sit on the ground with me. Think.

COMMENTARY

Peter Craven

It's not hard to imagine that Germaine Greer's *Quarterly Essay, Whitefella Jump Up* will draw fire from every side. Here we have the spectacle of an eminent expatriate, long nurtured by the fame that Australia in itself cannot give (much as it may contribute more than its fair share), lecturing her countrymen on why Aboriginality should be central to their sense of themselves and the nation they must construct or imagine into being if they are not to remain bemired in what she takes to be a legacy of their British colonial past with nothing but the spectre of American-style materialism and a parallel vassaldom to put in its place.

She shows little sympathy for the effort of white liberals in the direction of Reconciliation which she may take to be a shibboleth or a delusion, nor is she preoccupied here with the practical question of how to improve the material conditions of Aboriginal people that currently preoccupies Aborigine leaders like Noel Pearson (who have their own intolerance of the fruits of white liberalism). She does not engage directly with Robert Manne-style outrage at the wrongs done to the stolen generations of Aboriginal children, nor is she preoccupied with the debates between Henry Reynolds, on the one hand, and Keith Windschuttle, on the other, about the number of blacks who were or were not massacred by white settlers. (It would not be hard to infer where Greer would position herself in this debate but consideration of it is not part of her emphasis.)

Germaine Greer is at pains to emphasise that she is not addressing the subject of what is wrong with the Aborigines and how this can be redressed. On the contrary, it is the malaise that afflicts white Australia which she believes can only be cured with black medicine. The dislocation and the depression which has desolated white Australians has its physical correlative in the looming environmental crisis but it has always been there as a persistent unease, a mute apprehension of bad faith.

Part of the logic of Germaine Greer's essay is to invert the logic of the stereotype. It is white Australia that always made alcohol into a nightmare, as if binge drinking were the only way these hopeless Australian men could weep at what they have done to their world. It is white Australians who have cursed the land they trod on and indulged in doomed projective fantasies about the emptiness at its core and it is white Australians who felt that they suffered some inner damnation of estrangement from the land.

The literary critic in Germaine Greer sees this as a version of the affective fallacy where what was projected on to the land was the guilt and shame of dispossessing a people we knew had a feeling for it that should have made them our debtors not our servants, and victims.

Sometimes the characteristic Australian melancholy about the land took the form of the Irish pose of heroic survival but in fact the only way whites could live in this country was by trusting to the kindness and the know-how of the Aborigines. Even the bush narratives like Mary Durack's *Kings in Grass Castles* make this clear. Where would Patrick Durack have been without his Aboriginal retainer who in fact ran the station and was cherished but only as a lower form of life?

Germaine Greer is absolutely convincing in the way she handles the literary and historical stories of the depth of dependence of white and black as well as the depth (and self-mutilation) in the poignancy that attends the betrayal of the bond.

It's there in her account of the Lawson story about the white boy who would like to be a tracker like his black mate even though going native is anathema and a form of death. And in the end he's left to drift in a culture which has no language even to apprehend his grief.

Part of the image of Germaine Greer is a little like Gertrude Stein's description of Ezra Pound as "a village explainer. Excellent if you are a village. If not, not." A problem which can be compounded by the fact that Australia is the village she came from, long ago, and she has sometimes seemed to address it as if it were a village still. But if Australia remains something of a village, it's worth cottoning on to the fact that Greer is being the opposite of hectoring in what she is saying to this country. Her message is a message of mercy, not of vengeance. Hence her central suggestion that we admit we have been living in an Aboriginal country all along and that we should look in the mirror and tell ourselves where we are and what we are.

The idea of the Aborigines as mirror images of white Australians, the idea of all Australians seeing themselves in the mirror of Aboriginality, may seem strange to liberal-minded people who are acutely aware of the degradations that have been inflicted on the blacks but Germaine Greer seems to suggest that at least the willingness to identify is a matter of choice. She is careful not to speak for the blacks themselves but she emphasises that we must imagine a community before we can construct one. Aboriginality, for her, is not a matter of lines of descent, of genes and blood, it is a getting of wisdom and of understanding. What we have to understand is that the Aboriginal character of Australia is the best thing about the place, in a deep sense it is the only thing about the place that is worth believing in as a mythology and therefore we should cleave to it as an imaginative destiny, our national hope.

She appears to believe that as long as we conceive of the Aborigines as the thing we are not, the contrast that defines us, there will be no grace in us, no matter how theoretically liberal and well-disposed we may be.

This is heady stuff and it owes something to Benedict Anderson's notion of ideal (because imagined) communities but this kind of vision, and the audacity with which Greer argues so strenuously for it, may be precisely the kind of thing Australia has been yearning for all these years.

After all, as Greer says, the Aborigines have always been trying to seduce white Australians into their web of dreams and she emphasises not only the gentleness and kindliness of so much of the Aboriginal treatment of white Australians but also, in a speculative way, the affinities and influences which she suggests may flow from blacks to whites, not vice versa. Do the Aborigines really speak like a broader version of the British settlers or is the Australian accent with its nasalisation and pattering consonants mediated through a thousand black women nursing white settler children? And there are broad affinities of cultural empathy or of empathies that seem to go beyond "culture" narrowly conceived. What is the origin of Australian evasiveness, of our laconic character, our distaste for self-revelation and our love of endless yarning and anecdote?

When Cathy Freeman sat on the ground, after her great victory, wasn't that gesture something we instinctively understood in our bones and didn't we know, without thinking about it, that she was one of our own, not because of a derivative "Australia" as we currently conceive it, but because she was in the deepest sense *our* countrywoman and knew the land as her own?

Many pragmatic political Australians of every colour will dismiss this sort of thing as romantic, as the merest flag-flying of a symbolic politics but, as Don Watson said once, no one has ever successfully refuted the idealist view of history and if we are to change the direction of our history then a symbolism, grounded in experience, is our best hope.

Greer is scathing – some will think too hastily – about the way the Anglo-Celtic, up-yours-with-the-rent monoculture rapidly evacuates any of the potential of the multiculturalism we feign to believe in, but surely she has a point when she says that Aboriginality is the one thing that stands against Australianism in its current market-rules American mode?

Constitutional lawyers may wring their hands at what she says about the British crown as an absentee landlord but surely there is a symbolic logic in displacing this with the notion of land held by an Aboriginal republic in the name of the Australian people who define themselves as Aboriginal?

At times Greer sounds as if she thinks Aboriginality could translate us into a nation that identified, at least in its core values, in its central myth, with the people of the third world and she would see this as a great kick at British pomp and circumstance and the driving power of American domination.

Many years ago at the time of the dismissal of the Whitlam government, Germaine Greer said that Australia could have been the wonder of the earth because it could have been a nation built on prosperity that paid homage to a political vision that ministered to the poor of the earth. In many ways *Whitefella Jump Up* and the political vision it enunciates seems a continuation of that thought.

In one way Germaine Greer seems to be talking about something as heartening and manifest as the New Zealand identification with the Maori, with the thrill of pride, more powerful than colonialism, which fills the air when the All-Blacks, white and Maori, perform the haka. In another way she is suggesting we should simply sit upon the ground and listen to the stories our own earth tells. This is not a hectoring essay, nor a grandstanding one, and the reader would do well to set aside whatever she thinks of Germaine Greer.

It is a lucidly simple essay. It is an essay that refuses to presume, to buy into the rhetoric of the politics of the Aboriginal Question. At the same time it is an essay which crystallises something which has been in the air in this country for a long time now, what has often been vaguely thought but which has never, I think, been so well expressed.

Whitefella Jump Up is within an inch of not being a political essay at all but is, in the end, a political essay and a profound one. It is an essay about sitting down and thinking where all the politics start and what kind of legend Australia wants to place at its heart.

Peter Craven *is the editor at* Quarterly Essay. *This piece first appeared as the introduction to the autumn 2003 issue*

RESPONSES

LES MURRAY

At question time in a reading I gave in Cambridge a few years ago, a lady up the back row asserted, "You've got an Aboriginal accent!"

"It could well be, ma'am," I replied truthfully, though with doubts about her ear, "I've got any number of Aboriginal relatives." As possibly a majority of country Australians do.

When the audience and I were leaving, another woman asked me in awed tones, "Did you know who that was?" I said no, and she reverently uttered the name of Germaine Greer.

"I used to see her around Sydney University a long time

ago, but we never met," I told the English woman, not adding that I'd thought Dr Greer formidable and rather forbidding back then.

"Would you like to meet her now?" the woman asked breathlessly. I agreed that it was high time, and in the event Dr Greer and I got along amicably, like old contemporaries. I told her how I'd been moved by her book *Daddy, We Hardly Knew You*, which works like a fine novel. Whether she had been testing me to see whether I would fumble my response to her assertion and so maybe reveal a streak of racism, I guess I'll never know. Perhaps it was unworthy of me to entertain the suspicion, but these are horribly political times, as the very early '60s at Sydney were blessedly not.

One side of Dr Greer's new manifesto *Whitefella Jump Up* that strongly appeals to me is its subtle understanding of what for a generation I have been calling convergence, the slow mutual assimilation of Aborigines and other Australians. She understands the dynamics of this, how it is both genetic and cultural, and how truly equal it has been, despite all the efforts, earlier and recent, to hide and deny it. She is good on the Aboriginal visual art of the last thirty years, which for me is Australia's equivalent of jazz, a major new art style arising from the most oppressed group in our nation. The rest of her case mainly reflects the mythology of the Skippy left, and so will seem unreal to ethnic and mainstream Australia.

I doubt her proposal to transfer the nominal ownership of our country from Queen Elizabeth to the Aboriginal people, necessarily without any alteration of real ownerships, would have much chance in a referendum. I will be fascinated to read what Aboriginal citizens think of it. To me, it seems very American, in its urgent desire for resolution, for closure, the Big Fix Right Now, rather than the slow working out of themes and equity in a society. Something like it, if genuinely and widely embraced, might secure more visibility and credit for Aborigines as a vital creative force among us and a potent source of subconscious iconography. But a new consciousness of Aboriginal culture and art may have already brought this, in the wider community. In a poem I wrote two or three years back, I adverted to what must surely be a marvel of serendipity, if indeed the architect didn't study Aboriginal forms:

Clothing as Dwelling as Shouldered Boat

Propped sheets of bark converging
over skin-oils and a winter fire,
stitched hides of furry rug-cloak

with their naked backs to the weather,
clothing as dwelling as shouldered boat
beetle-backed, with bending ridgelines,
all this, resurrected and gigantic:
the Opera House,
Sydney's Aboriginal building.

Les Murray*'s latest book in Australia is* Learning Human: New Selected Poems *(Duffy & Snellgrove, 2003).*

LILLIAN HOLT

Every now and again, somebody arrives in town to lift my flagging spirits.

In this case, it was Germaine Greer. I went to see her at the *Quarterly Essay* launch where she talked about her ideas on black/white relations in this country.

As I listened to her, I was buoyed, bowled over, by her boldness. In a country which treads cautiously in case anybody gets upset about the issues – especially whitefellas – I wanted to clap every word she uttered.

Immediately, I went up to her after her speech and said, "You know, Germaine, I'd walk a million miles to hear a whitefella like yourself say what you said here just now. I've been trying to teach about Whiteness for ages. That is, to get whitefellas to look at themselves and not keep researching, studying and labelling us any more."

But caution: Don't ask me exactly what she said to prompt my response. Don't ask me exactly what she wrote. All I know is that it resonated with me. It gave me hope. It replenished my spirit. It spoke to my condition and that of this country. It inspired and fired me up.

Next day, I heard and saw her being interviewed on TV

and radio. The interviewers wanted to know what she meant exactly by an Australian Aboriginal Republic. To which she replied, "I don't know."

Don't know! Now what kind of answer is that, Germaine, in a country where everyone knows about or at least has an opinion on the original inhabitants? There was dead silence and astonishment on the part of the interviewers. Followed by nervous laughter with a faltering "but you're the one suggesting it!"

"Yes," said Germaine. "I just want to put it out there for people to think about it."

Pregnant pause on part of interviewer. Then move on to next question.

I thought to myself, Good on you, Germaine – finally a whitefella who can admit to "not knowing". In this quantitative, measured, controlled society we live in, where one is expected "to know" at all times, at all costs, where there are so many "experts" on Aborigines, it's refreshing to hear such an august and audacious academic say, "I don't know."

I hadn't heard whitefellas talking like this for a long time. And my spirit was in sore need of succour. The last time I got such a hit of hope was from Jane Elliott in 1997 just after a rather nasal-voiced, mean-spirited, suburban redhead from Ipswich emerged.

Thank God there are such people as Jane and Germaine

who will say such things. Provoke. Confront the complacency. It has to come from them. It can't come from us mob because we get labelled as "carping boongs or whingeing blackfellas" if we as much as confront/criticise this rich and abundant but racialised country in which we live.

It has to come from the power and privilege of Whiteness which both women both inhabit, daily.

Germaine Greer picked up lots of "brownie points" (no pun intended) from me and my fellow blackfella mate Gary Thomas. We were the only two Aboriginal people present at the launch.

I said to him as we left, "What did you think of Germaine Greer?"

Without hesitation, he said, "I really liked her because she is not afraid to dream … and to dream big, Lill."

What an accolade from an Aborigine!

And, yes, I agree!

We need to dream, dream big, dream this country into full existence.

And, like Germaine, don't ask me exactly what I mean by that. Just go away and think about it!

Lillian Holt *is a University of Melbourne Fellow. She is the former Director of the Centre of Indigenous Education at the University of Melbourne.*

P.A. DURACK CLANCY

Commonsense dictates: ignore Germaine Greer's latest attention-seeking stunt. Response will simply encourage her. Reaction, it seems, is just what the "eminent expatriate" awaits.

It is possible to ignore the main thrust of Greer's essay – her admonition to whitefellas to become jumped-up born-again blackfellas. Let those who will "sit on the ground with [Greer] and think". Others will give her nought out of ten for workable short cuts; ten out of ten for media coverage.

It is even possible to ignore the numerous comments that reveal the depth of Greer's myopia regarding Australia's past and present. On page 35, for instance: "[in 1971] half a world away ... I could suddenly see that what was operating in Australia was apartheid ..." More comparable "insights", along with contradictions galore, appear throughout the essay.

It is possible, too, to ignore the few occasions where Greer actually says something that is correct. The sentence beginning: "The intervention of the academics ..." on page 75, is one such instance.

It is simply not possible, however, to ignore what Greer has to say when she turns her careless sights and shoots venom upon Mary Durack's Australian classic *Kings in Grass Castles.*

Greer is not the first to descend upon *Kings* and willy-nilly to pluck passages from it in support of some specious thesis.

Indeed for the past twenty years or so various minnows have nibbled at *Kings.* Those of us who happen, with reason, to admire our forebears' achievements and Mary Durack's art as a writer and historian may have been irritated by the minnows but most of the time the things they said were so absurd and wide of the mark they could not be taken very seriously.

When "a renowned writer, academic and broadcaster", quite a big fish in other words, also attacks *Kings* and Duracks and comes up with even more absurd and offensive inaccuracies than the minnows, it is time to stop thinking that the abuse of Australian history and of our family will simply go away.

As far as I am concerned there is no point in enumerating all of Greer's shameless misrepresentations of *Kings*, its author and its lead characters. Three examples of the way Greer distorts history and of her jaundiced slipshod method will suffice.

The examples come from a long paragraph beginning on page 108 with, "The evidence from the Durack family ..." and concluding on page 110 with "... an expensive disaster". In amongst this jumbled paragraph Greer says:

> 1. "In 1879 their land hunger drove a posse of Durack men westwards towards the Kimberley where ... they helped themselves to the pick of the Ord and Fitzroy country ..."

In these remarks Greer summarises about five detailed chapters of *Kings*. Fair enough to condense, but what rough research led to such distortion of the facts? Apparently Greer cares not a jot for accuracy. In the interests of the latter, and for the record, here is a factual account of Greer's loaded sentence above.

In July 1882, following reports by Alexander Forrest of his 1879 expedition to Kimberley, a party of six men, "expert bushmen of proven toughness and resource" led by "Stumpy" Michael Durack, left Brisbane by sea with "twenty-three tried and well-bred horses" and fifteen hundredweight of rations and equipment. They were bound for Cambridge Gulf, Western Australia to see for themselves whether the Kimberley country was as favourable and suitable for stock as Forrest had claimed. In Darwin they engaged two Aborigines, Pannikin and Pintpot, who not only proved their worth on the expedition but so relished their Durack experience they later joined the team on the long trek that led Queensland cattle into Kimberley.

In short, Greer's "land-hungry posse" was a well-organised, well-disciplined reconnaissance, or survey, party composed of white and black men.

2. In the same paragraph, page 110, Greer adds: "[the Duracks'] first expedition [to Kimberley] was a disaster and they were repeatedly lost on the second ..."

Again, for the record: In 1879 Alexander Forrest had "conjectured" that the mouth of the Ord was on the west of Cambridge Gulf and that is where the Durack survey party first landed in August 1882. It needs to be noted that before this date the rivers of East Kimberley had not been mapped. (Nor were there any roads, let alone comfy air-conditioned four-wheel drives that today's "Kimberley explorers" take for granted. It should not be necessary to spell all this out but apparently it is for the likes of Greer.) Stumpy Michael and his party were identifying rivers and naming them for whitefella maps. They were the first to start sketching on paper the river courses and their tributaries. Over time it was discovered that five major rivers flow into Cambridge Gulf. The Ord had been named by Forrest but its course was not known. Stumpy Michael, foreseeing the route to the Ord would be circuitous, marked a boab tree "D1" at the site of their first camp. Within one month of landing on the west side of Cambridge Gulf the Durack party had found the Ord some two hundred kilometres east at its junction with the Negri (as noted by Forrest). There they marked a final boab "D24", followed the river downstream almost to its mouth and reported Kimberley country to be "fine beyond expectations ..."

Their return route, still "in the saddle", was some one thousand kilometres west to Beagle Bay. From there they caught a ship to Fremantle and another on to Brisbane. From start to finish the reconnaissance took six months. It achieved its principal aim: to sight and assess land before commitment to leasing. Eleven horses had been lost but there had been no loss of human life – white or black. By any normal reckoning this first expedition was remarkably successful.

Yet Greer in her ivory tower at the University of Warwick sweepingly dismisses the expedition as "a disaster"? Has she ever read *Kings*?

Or did she pass on the task to some clueless research assistant? More likely, she uncritically accepted and repeated the denigrations of the minnows.

As for "they [the Duracks] were repeatedly lost on their second expedition [to Kimberley] ..." This remark is Greer's view of the 1883–1885 overland cattle drive from Queensland through the Territory to East Kimberley. Has she any realistic understanding of moving stock long distances through uncharted land? Her put-down of the epic achievement is beneath contempt.

> 3. Greer again, on page 109: "The Duracks understood so little of what they were doing in the Kimberley they couldn't even position their original dwelling at Argyle high enough to escape the rising waters of the Behn River in the wet season ... it doesn't take much bushcraft to find evidence of periodic flood; evidently they didn't even look ..."

What an offensive and inaccurate view of those "first footers" who shared a reputation with the finest bushmen in the land. Sure the Behn rose high in the record wet of 1888 and the kitchen, built as was customary well separate from the main house, was swept away. The house itself, however, withstood the flood and remained in use as a functioning homestead on the place where my great-grandfather Patsy and Pumpkin pegged it until it was drowned by the waters of Lake Argyle some ninety years later – (another story ...)

While ever "posses" of prejudiced influential academics set out to rewrite our history and to knock cherished and good Australian stories (I refer not only to *Kings*), what hope for "reconciliation"? What hope too when loopy negative cock and bull is condoned and applauded? It would be interesting to know, for instance, the number of Australians who would agree that Greer's "vision ... may be precisely the kind of thing Australia has been yearning for all these years"; or that *Whitefella Jump Up* "crystallises something which has been in the air ... for a long time ... but which has never ... been so well expressed"? My tip is that if today's battlers were ever to read the essay it would (to paraphrase Greer) simply confirm their own deserved loathing of the eggheads.

For those of us who live in Australia there has long been awareness that in many subtle ways aspects of Aboriginal culture impinge on our lives. Likewise there is a mostly easygoing awareness and acceptance of many other peoples' cultures. If being Australian is something that we feel and know "in our bones", why try to pin it down? Can identity be pinned down? Surely identity, personal and national, is a dynamic concept that meanders, changes and adjusts as circumstances and understandings evolve?

To conclude with a prayer: Please God, spare us from a zealous self-exiled academic who preaches to us in real old-style missionary mode that "the way to light is through darkness, and this darkest hour could be just before our dawn as a genuinely new nation ..." Amen.

P.A. Durack Clancy *has worked as a curator, gallery owner and teacher in Australia and abroad. Currently she manages the artistic estate of her mother, Elizabeth Durack. She is a niece of Mary Durack, author of* Kings in Grass Castles.

FAY ZWICKY

Yet another of Greer's unanswerable self-explorations, the essay can hardly be accorded the kind of profundity or logic claimed for it by Peter Craven in his introduction. Nor do I think it either simple or resistant to the "politics of the Aboriginal Question" – have we read the same piece? To attempt to argue a coherent case either against or for would be as futile as repudiating a novel or film for imaginative excess or praising both for political correctness.

However sympathetic to the spirit of the cause at the heart of what is essentially a polemical *apologia*, I feel that Greer strains to enlarge into broader cultural relevance the dimensions of something entirely personal: her own sense of loss and displacement. As daughter of the priestly utterance with a vision of the ideal, her posture of defender of the dispossessed is theatrically compelling if impracticable. So it's pointless to argue with such imaginative forays in which nobody with any idea of the complexity of what's at stake would presume to lay claim to a moral high ground, least of all those whom she has set out to champion.

In 1996, I wrote that "Greer has rarely embarked on a

project without energetic recourse to private demons and their exorcism." In her customary cat-among-the-pigeons style, speaking out of the usual anxiety of exile, she again goes looking for a place of belonging, an authentic home to return to in order to reckon with what has made her. In so doing, she faithfully mirrors what she's discerned as her culture's shortcomings even as she mocks them.

In 1989, I also said that "her inconsistencies and dependence on stereotypes are endearing when they aren't irritating, limiting, as they do, the undeveloped emotional potential of her formidable intelligence". My opinion hasn't changed since reading *Whitefella Jump Up* despite my sympathy for and admiration of her quixotic courage. I don't presume to know what the Aborigines she sat down with on her mattress under the river gums thought about her. My guess is that their infallible courtesy would have precluded anything other than the sort of kindly dispassionate reassurance and confirmation so clearly needed by this funny visitor. The Aborigines I've met have no desire to sit on the ground: they're far too preoccupied helping others, trying to educate themselves and their children for existence in a difficult world like the rest of us.

Learning that there are situations admitting no easy solution, questions for which answers aren't readily available, comes hard to most people, and maybe harder still to the intellectually gifted and articulate in a non-verbal culture. I know because, six years older than Greer, I've been there myself and been suitably chastened into scepticism. It doesn't mean that one gives up on hope or change. Rather, it means taking smaller, less heroic steps as many are doing, unsung and far removed from media attention and public homage. There are no short cuts to anything worthwhile, let alone that much-abused and little understood concept "nationhood".

Towards the end of a life also armoured in a clever acerbic intellect, James McAuley wrote a poem about his parents called "Because", revealing a hard-won wisdom that refused to exaggerate, sentimentalise or mythicise. Cold comfort perhaps, but I'll let the last two stanzas act as a classicist's reply to Greer's hunger for the ideal:

> Judgment is simply trying to reject
> A part of what we are because it hurts.
> The living cannot call the dead collect;
> They won't accept the charge, and it reverts.
>
> It's my own judgment day that I draw near,
> Descending in the past without a clue,

Down to that central deadness: the despair
Older than any hope I ever knew.

Good as it is to be reminded of the ideal, I'm afraid Greer's gadfly vision is beyond possibility. To be drawn to it, take it to heart but understand that one's endeavours are, however successful in the temporal sense, inevitably failures, is to acknowledge the human condition in its starkest monochrome aspect. Living in present-day Australia is not a bad way to get, as the young say, real.

Fay Zwicky*'s books include* Kaddish and Other Poems *(1982),* Ask Me *(1990) and* Poems 1970–1993*. Her most recent book,* The Gatekeeper's Wife, *was published by Brandl & Schlesinger in 1997.*

MARCIA LANGTON

Germaine Greer's *Whitefella Jump Up* proposes a whimsical solution to the immaturity and rawness of Australian nationhood and national identity. In her extended lament for "white" Australia's lack of a sense of belonging to its expropriated homeland, she contends that if white Australians could accept their "ineradicable and inherent Aboriginality" (this "characteristic of the continent itself"), they will be "truly self-governing and independent". Greer is embarrassed by persistent genuflections towards the British and the Americans, exasperated with the specious British ethnicity to which many "white" Australians cling, and disappointed by their failure to forge a full-blown identity that would anchor them in this continent. She wants Australians to acknowledge formally, in a nation-remaking gesture, that they have inherited an assortment of Aboriginal characteristics absorbed by their frontier forefathers in close and friendly contact with Aboriginal people.

I do not subscribe to the view that expatriates have no right to enunciate their views about the state of the homeland, but the niggling doubt about Greer's depth of engagement with matters at home frays my commitment to the right to free speech in this case. Essentialist ideas about identity – for instance that a person's or a nation's identity is shaped by "race" – have permeated Australian life since the idea of an Australian nation was invented in the late nineteenth century. Simply to flip the foundation of the nation from a fundamentally White identity to a Black one is to remain trapped by the racism on which the nation was founded in 1901. Alfred Deakin judged that the strongest motive for federation was "the desire that we should be one people, and remain one people, without the admixture of other races". Race was a key constitutional issue in 1900 when the drafters of the Australian Constitution excluded Aborigines from the ambit of this founding document in order to prevent surviving post-frontier Aboriginal populations from affecting the parliamentary representation of the states and financial distributions by the Commonwealth to the states. In a recent case the High Court of Australia has found that one of its provisions can be read in such a way as to permit government actions that work to the detriment of Aboriginal people. Admitted neither as nations nor as citizens, Aboriginal peoples have been the subjects of an extraordinary history of policy experimentation, much of it predicated on the belief that the first Australians would disappear.

What is astonishing about Dr Greer's essay is the absence of any substantial reference to the "big picture" ideas for a post-colonial Australia during the last decade and their defeat at the polls by neo-conservatives who lured the electorate into voting against an Australian head of state and abhorred the idea of reconciliation with Aborigines together with Keating-style engagement with Asia and the Pacific. The history of removing Aboriginal children from their families is briefly mentioned, but this is incidental to a curiously over-emphasised sexual history of the Australian nation. One might read Greer's main contention as a way of bypassing just how ugly the rejection of the "big picture" was – this was the period marked by Pauline Hanson's rise to fame – and of holding instead to a brighter vision in order to beguile readers with nice arguments that draw on evidence from Australian literature, that speculate on the influence of Aboriginal languages on the Australian way of talking and on the origin in Aboriginal culture of the supposed Australian preference for egalitarianism.

Were the arguments and the vision itself more persuasive, the essay might be a serious challenge to the severely diminished idea of the nation presently proposed by contenders from both the Right and the Left. But Greer seems to be ignorant of an enormous body of fictional and nonfictional writing, cinema and art that has tackled this topic in a variety of regions and periods. For instance, she seems to have failed to notice that the last three decades have produced a body of historical literature which has made possible a much more robust idea of the past from which Australians need not shrink in denial, but which, if wrestled with honestly, lays the foundations for a new story of the nation. But there are also some particularly vicious ideas circulating at present which reinforce the old myth of a nation forged, so the assertion goes, by God-fearing men of restraint. As a consequence, this profoundly important new literature is presently under heavy attack by Keith Windschuttle and other patriotic warriors from the *Quadrant* fold who claim to be concerned with the craft of history, but these matters appear not to concern Dr Greer.

While Greer's idea is a far more pleasant one than that proposed by the present prime minister in his 1996 Menzies Lecture, it is just as tendentious. Where Howard's view of the nation's history is expedient, with its forelock-tugging to Brave Pioneers and Little Aussie Battlers traduced and silenced by the brigade of wicked, black armband-wearing thought police, Greer's idea is a weak tonic for this shallowness of identity, treating the infirmity with symbolic medicine rather than efficacious antidote. Where Howard was concerned "to ensure that our history as a nation is not written definitively by those who take the view that Australians should apologise for most of it", Greer has drafted an idea of the nation that equally circumvents the horrible fate of Aboriginal people during that history, and for which some act of restitution from the settler state, such as an apology, is still required, if only to state an intention to refuse to allow such acts to happen again. This, I believe, is the secret at the heart of all the sneakily coded references to the idea of the nation expressed by opponents of Patrick Dodson's vision: their motives are dubious. Or, at least, that is the threat that hovers before those of us who embrace our Aboriginality with pride.

The greatest weakness of Germaine Greer's essay is its zany disconnectedness. Aboriginal societies were pushed to the brink of extinction, and yet the evidence for the Aboriginal influence on Australia culture is valorised in Greer's essay with no mention of the disappearance of Aboriginal languages and the loss of cultural knowledge with the passing of the last generations who were brought up in the bush. For instance, her argument that the Australian accent derives from Aboriginal nannies teaching white children to speak and Aboriginal people influencing their white mates' nasalised vowels as they yarned around the campfire is an example of simple inductivism, fitting a few scraps of literary evidence to feminist psychological theory. The comments about the influence of "corroborees" on Australian history are fascinating but not sufficiently supported by the evidence presented (though there is evidence, some of which is discussed in Henry Reynolds' *With the White People*).

While Greer's literary training allows her to sustain such romantic, if eccentric notions, linguistic research tells us that the 250 Aboriginal languages that existed at the time of British settlement have been reduced to less than fifty. All but a handful of Aboriginal languages will be extinct within fifty years. This is largely because Aboriginal people were forced to speak English instead of their own languages. With the exception of a few missionaries and linguists, few Australians have learnt to speak an Aboriginal language. Aboriginal children were not allowed to speak their native tongues at school and were punished for doing so. Aboriginal languages are the truly Australian languages, and constitute a precious heritage. Conserving Aboriginal languages by teaching them in schools in the vicinity of the relevant linguistic communities would be a splendid Australian gesture in the right direction. If *Whitefella Jump Up* has a lasting value it might lie in the power of Greer's appeal to Australians to embrace Aboriginal culture as their own. There has been plenty of cultural diffusion in Australian history as in any other. The impetus for Australians to value Aboriginal culture might arise from a sense of this culture as being a part of their own heritage and their own historical legacy, not just that of exoticised and demonised others.

In the search for a sense of gravitas to underpin their "national identity", Australians seem doomed to suffer one caricature after another, one more "prawn on the barbie", one more cry from the heart and yet another diagnosis of the imagined crisis. All the while, of course, there have been some appealing and singular expositions of common themes, some of them textured and nuanced in the articulation, in the ideas about what it means to belong to a nation.

As Hugh Mackay and other students of the "national mood" attest, there is a far greater variegation and complexity to the construction of the "Nation" than newspaper columnists, politicians and ideologues ever dream of. And there is a dizzying range of differences – generational, regional, economic, educational, ethnic, cultural – to contend with. Greer's vision of Australians somehow coming to adopt "their" Aboriginality is simply at odds with the facts of life in our country today. It's a vision that expresses the needy idealism of the baby-boomer generation, one of waning relevance to the younger generations of Australian intellectuals who lack the sentimentalism of Greer and her cohort and who are assuming ascendancy in public life.

With their access to a global market that empowers them as more than mere consumers, younger urban Australians are cyber-citizens, at once cosmopolitan and networked. They are able to relate to the Aboriginal world in a less troubled way than their parents and they are almost oblivious to Australia's blinding colonial legacy of white supremacy and race hatred. Their images of the Aboriginal world are not the images of monochromatic misery that their parents see, but a heady mix of politics, sport and culture. They are familiar with a pageant of Aboriginal people who are talented, capable and attractive and who function as filmmakers, musicians, dancers, artists, writers, sports stars, intellectuals and actors. The reality and variety of the Aboriginal world is available to them as it never was to their parents. And for that reason they do not need to invent an Australia wrapped up in Aboriginal symbolism. But I do not want to overstate the case. They are less tolerant of the welfare approach to Aboriginal disadvantage, though they are also, to be fair, less niggardly than their parents' generation. They are arguably the true advocates of the "fair go", because their sense of fairness tells them that everyone should take responsibility for their own fate to the extent that they can. To this extent, Noel Pearson represents the views of a younger Australia as much as he represents those of young Aboriginal people.

The national literature of the '60s lecture hall

Greer's heavy reliance on "classical" Australian literary fiction is redolent of the late 1960s and the sense of protest at the colonial legacy of Australian literature. She critiques the references to Aboriginal people in Henry Lawson, Tom Collins and Mary Durack, and finds fair deeds and foul. Like Toni Morrison on Mark Twain, she does a good job of exposing one-eyed racism and of exalting the humanity of people who come alive on the pages of literature without the ideological drag of "race". But it's a limited sense of Australian literary history Greer exhibits. True, she cites Frank Moorhouse, Thomas Keneally, Sally Morgan, Mudrooroo, Tim Flannery and other modern writers, but we are left with the distinct impression that Australian literary life shrivelled after she left Sydney for London. What about David Malouf (*The Conversations at Curlow Creek*), Richard Flanagan (*Death of a River Guide*), Tim Winton (*Dirt Music*), Rodney Hall (*The Island in the Mind* trilogy),

Murray Bail (*Eucalyptus*)? Apparently, Greer has not noticed that a distinctive Australian settler voice that speaks of a deepening attachment to place and locality as the core of identity has emerged in Australian literature. While Greer boasts of her adoption by people of the Kulin nation, other Australians are trying hard to adopt their own backyards and take responsibility for their history, their environment and the inheritance of their own racism. Books such as Nicholas Rothwell's *Wings of the Kite-Hawk*, Peter Read's *Belonging: Australians, Place and Aboriginal Ownership*, Eric Rolls' *A Million Wild Acres* and George Seddon's *Landprints: Reflections on Place and Landscape* attest to the various degrees of success Australians have had in explaining their intimate and variegated relationships with place, locality and history. The point is that the Aboriginal attachment to places, inherited from many generations of ancestors and shaped by kinship, descent, culture and religion, does not preclude settlers from engaging with the land they love. Is it really necessary to claim a few threads of Aboriginality in order to affirm that experience? Might it not be more honourable to acknowledge frankly the frontier history that gave the white Australians their ascendancy, their control of the land and resources that have made them so wealthy. In this respect James Boyce's essay in Robert

Manne's recent collection *Whitewash* is crucially important. Boyce tackles Keith Windschuttle's nasty tome, *The Fabrication of Aboriginal History: Volume One.* His conclusion suggests the sheer difficulty involved in the debate about the character of the Australian nation and the complexity of the responsibility involved, towards whites as well as Aborigines:

> Many will understandably want to ignore Windschuttle's book dismissing it as either very bad academic history or a poisonous political tract, both of which are true. But in the end, the Tasmanian community will need to find a language and a framework – as other groups have been forced to do – to deal with the material in the text that is not concerned with academic debate but constitutes a slander on the custodians and creators of our land. This is not just up to Aborigines or activists: some respect for those almost-timeless generations who lived and developed this island before us is surely beyond race or politics; it simply flows from a love of the place.

While Dr Greer's essay proposes a way for Australians to engage with Australia as a homeland, however ludicrous her central idea may seem, it is at least a vision that does not spring from hate. But it does skim lightly over the surface of the troubling issues Boyce contends with, and while it would be churlish to say that her essay is insulting, it nevertheless is necessary to say that the ease of her solution is exasperating in its triviality.

If Australians are concerned about national identity, then it seems to me that the history of Aboriginal–settler relations is as good a place as any to search for something worth constructing. But what can we make of what our intellectuals find in their quest for a history? Greer finds such commonality between Aborigines and "whites" that she recommends that "white" people declare their nation Aboriginal. Windschuttle finds only the most primitive people on earth, incapable of owning land, who seem to have asked for it so that it was the most natural thing in the world that they should die out. The challenge is there in these two facile conclusions. It is the challenge for settler Australians of recognising that Aboriginal people are fully human beings and the further challenge of recognising the value in the differences between our cultures and societies in such a way that everyone can own the civil society we share and, if you like, the "national identity" we yearn for with an equal cause and an equal commitment. This challenge goes under the label of "Reconciliation".

But we should be fair to Germaine Greer. Even if her essential idea is flawed with a romantic notion of race, Dr Greer's contribution throws into stark relief some of the myths that underpin the difficulty of overcoming the inherited frontier hatred that continues to drive racist discourse in Australian public life. Her essay leaves me pondering the question of whether, in the end, a post-colonial patriotism is even possible. Is it possible that Australians will one day recognise the nations enclosed within their Commonwealth, the Aboriginal and Torres Strait Islander nations from whose homelands a recreant and uncomprehending nation has been carved?

Marcia Langton *has published extensively on Aboriginal affairs issues. She is Professor of Australian Indigenous Studies at the University of Melbourne.*

TONY BIRCH

It would not be difficult to dismiss Germaine Greer's *Whitefella Jump Up*. Several commentators have already done so, with aggressive relish. Her essay is not only forearmed for ridicule, it predicts it. And in consideration of Greer's feistiness, I am sure that it welcomes it.

The writing in *Whitefella* does highlight some of Greer's faults. Its engagement with contemporary Australian political and cultural life is at times vague and is reliant on highly questionable generalisations, while its reading of Australia's colonial past leads to some poorly considered conclusions. For instance, Greer explains some of the psychological forces that drove early colonial violence and acts of dispossession in Australia as a result of "the British elite" having quite possibly "caught the madness from the Irish". This particular madness turns out to be a pathology that denied both the *legal* and human presence of indigenous peoples in Australia and was born of the effects of the dispossession and subjugation of the Irish themselves by the British in their homeland.

The British didn't need the Irish or any other colonised nation to teach them the art of violent conquest. Nor was their adherence to the preposterous notion of terra nullius (reproduced *ad nauseam* through narratives of denial) fed by any madness or ignorance. This interpretation was the invention of melancholic poets and novelists, their inspiration being that peculiar form of imperialist nostalgia present in Western colonial societies from the mid-nineteenth century and arising in the period following the "successful" conquest of the invaded.

When the British aristocrat Granville William Chetwynd Stayplton accompanied the Chief Surveyor of the colony of New South Wales, Major Thomas Mitchell, through what was to become the western district of Victoria in 1836, he wrote that the land was "at present worth sixty millions to the Exchequer of England" and that it would result in a "good fat grant" for the discoverers (i.e. himself and Mitchell). This expedition ended with the murder of several indigenous men and the explorers' mapping of, and consequent claim to, the landscape that led to the widespread invasion of indigenous country. Greer's view of this period of colonial history, for all its apparent critical tone, in fact romanticises settler violence and ignores the more systematic, orderly and sanctioned processes of colonisation, which were fed more by the imperatives of capitalist/imperialist expansion than by any desire to reconstruct "home" that might spring from loneliness, emotional absence and anxiety.

And it would not be difficult to pick over *Whitefella Jump Up* and highlight other instances where Greer appears to lack a serious engagement with Australia, past and present. But to do so would be to ignore other aspects of the essay that I consider to be of value at a political moment when the status of indigenous communities in Australia has been pushed to the margins once more, led by a federal government determined to recolonise the indigenous body within a nominally post-colonial nation.

While the concluding sentence of Greer's essay consists of the single word "Think" it is clear that she is well aware that her comments will do little more than add to the tendency of some people in Australia to "think" that Germaine Greer is quite mad.

Greer may well be mad. But if we are going to have madness I prefer Greer's to that of those charged with the administration of this country's "commitment" to the rights of indigenous communities. Greer may be suffering from a provocative madness, a political, even a cheeky madness that will win her few friends. But better Greer's "craziness" (as she calls it) than the psychosis that continues to demean indigenous people in Australia and which enforces a proactive discrimination against indigenous people before informing those very people that their suffering and disadvantage is of their own making. The "Aboriginal problem" here is the creation of "the Aborigines" themselves, who have enacted their own dispossession because of their inherent laziness or dysfunctionalism.

It could also be argued that Greer's central thesis, that there is a need to "Aboriginalise" the Australian nation, is little more than a shallow appropriation of indigenous culture and identity. If interpreted literally, it is so, without doubt. Of itself, it is not a new idea. Manifestations of the "white Aborigine" have occurred throughout Australian history, sometimes as attempts to appropriate indigenous culture for commercial gain or to conjure into being a spiritual attachment and "belonging" to the land.

But Greer's proposal does more than this. She encourages white Australia to think beyond these merely comfortable constructions because of the explicitness with which she asks people to conceive of their "Aboriginality". It is the very impossibility and unlikelihood of the process of self-examination she suggests non-Aboriginal Australia undergo that could produce a constructive dialogue about identity in Australia and a new understanding of this country's history of colonialism. As an idea, as a utopian ideal (which may represent Greer's frustrated response to the current state of the nation), this central point of the essay may provide a needful stimulation to how we think of the psyche of non-Aboriginal Australia.

Greer directs her commentary to her "white countrymen", those whom she considers to be the problem, the obstacle to any attempt to facilitate Australia's development as a mature and inclusive nation. Therefore as an Aboriginal (and for once, as an "unproblematic" reader) I was most interested (and amused) to wonder how Greer's country folk would respond to her provocation that they take a good hard look at themselves in the mirror and repeat, "I live in an Aboriginal country." Once they get over the initial shock, she suggests that settler-Australians take a second look and convince themselves with this mantra that, "I was born in an Aboriginal country, therefore I must be considered Aboriginal."

It certainly sounds like stealing an indigenous identity. But Greer's challenge is both more astute and more subtle than that. I imagine that many people will want to dismiss Greer because they do not want to look in the mirror. And while a lot of them may not want to be "considered" Aboriginal in the true sense, they will find it discomforting to consider more closely their own identity and its complicity in the effort to dispossess indigenous people. I don't know if this was Greer's intention, nor do I think it matters whether it was or not.

She is, after all, responsible for the fact that I can let my imagination run with the prospect of how to bear witness to her invitation to the nation and what might be done in response. I would like to accept the role of the voyeur, or perhaps the psychiatrist who is allowed to hide behind the one-way mirror of colonialism and watch as a John Howard or a Pauline Hanson has to chant, "I live in an Aboriginal country … I live in an Aboriginal country." I wonder how "relaxed and comfortable" the Prime Minister would feel about that?

Not only would white Australia have to look at itself in Greer's mirror, it would have to look more directly at the face of black Australia as well. In the post-war era of the Aboriginal reserves and missions system in Victoria, the residents of the Lake Tyers Aboriginal Reserve in Gippsland were faced with a daily humiliation. The manager's office at the reserve was constructed in such a way that when people visited the manager they could not see his face while they stood at the enquiries desk. Because of an elaborate system of mirrors in the office the manager could see the Aboriginal people but they could not see him, they could not confront his image, and therefore the manager did not have to confront himself either.

Those who are prepared to do as Greer requests will not find their "Aboriginality" in the mirror. The exercise will not be a journey to what Greer imagines as "the shortest way to nationhood". But if the viewers are prepared to look closely enough they may see something that will at least present questions about what it really is that goes to make up "nationhood" and what sort of nation it is that allows its elected government to treat indigenous people the way that the Australian nation-state does. If the white Australian tries to find his Aboriginal face in the mirror, he may come to see his own face as the face of the oppressor.

In his most recent book, *Freedom Dreams: The Black Radical Imagination*, the African-American scholar Robin Kelley discusses aspects of the history of the black civil rights struggle in America with particular reference to some of the more utopian and idealistic sections of the movement. Kelley concludes his book with the articulation of his own "freedom dream"; he puts forward the idea that "ground zero", the site of the World Trade Center towers collapse in New York, should be an "international territory", that the land should "belong to the world and thus should not be privatized". The site would also stand as an emblem in recognition of Native American "first nations" people and would symbolically represent them as the people of the New York area. Kelley admits that his dream "will never happen without a struggle" but still he passionately defends his right to own "the space to imagine" and to create this "vision".

There is so little constructive vision in Australia at the moment. We are asked to provide sanctuary to those refugees who risk death in order to gain freedom for themselves and their families, and we respond with fences to keep them out and to lock them up. That is a seriously mad idea. Another one is the idea that indigenous communities who have had almost everything they possess taken from them should be asked to labour for next to no wages apart from subsistence dole money. That is not a visionary position. That is a new version of the poorhouse and it represents the rebirth of one of the most repressive ideas of the past.

So, with such architects of violence in mind, I have to acknowledge that Germaine Greer has provided this "dear reader" with a piece of strategic insanity that can infuriate and stimulate at the same time. Tomorrow morning when I look in the mirror before shaving I am going to repeat to myself, "You are living in a just society … You are living in a just society." I know that I will not believe myself. But I hope that the exercise at least makes me wonder what it is we should be doing to create that just society.

Tony Birch *is an historian and a writer of short fiction, poetry and creative non-fiction. He is co-author of* Reversing the Negative: A Portrait of Aboriginal Victoria.

MARY ELLEN JORDAN

Whitefella Jump Up. That's me Germaine Greer is talking to. Jump up? Up where? Ah – to the mystical higher plane of Aboriginality. Germaine Greer has cast herself as midwife to the rebirth of Australia and white Australians. Yes, we are to be born again – but not as clap-hands-for-Jesus Christians; not as crystal-toting new-agers; not as super-self-aware consumers of pop psychology; but in a history-defying move, leaping cultural differences in a single bound, white Australia is to be born again as Aboriginal.

What might this mean? Is it satire? Is it nonsense? Could it possibly be the commonsense Greer says it is?

Germaine Greer is famous for being outrageous, so it's no surprise that some of her claims in *Whitefella Jump Up* are a bit out there. But even if her basic premise doesn't hang together, we can still enjoy the ride and think about some of the things Greer says along the way. Did she expect us to take seriously her revised version of history in which the British attempt to colonise Australia has failed? For her, the failure of individual attempts at settling in various parts of Australia adds up to the failure of colonisation itself. This failure has left a whole lot of non-indigenous Australians stranded on the eastern shore of an Aboriginal land, where we first landed.

While Greer's account is clearly inaccurate, I did enjoy the inverted stories and rewritten histories such as this. They create an imagined world in which the power is reversed, any talk of assimilation is of white to black, and the only option non-Aboriginal people have for survival is to respectfully go to Aboriginal people to ask them how to live, and to hope desperately not to be turned away.

The imagined can make us see the real more clearly. The deserted interior that Greer encourages us to think of as the site of failed colonisation is in fact the site of multiple failures and multiple sorrows — the spectacular failures of white settlers to live harmoniously with Aboriginal people, and to respect them and learn from them; the blundering damage that has been done, and is still done, to the Australian environment; the fragmentation of Aboriginal families and communities; and the frontier violence. Colonisation failed in many things; but it did not fail to take hold.

As long as we assume that Greer is not to be read literally, this part of Greer's retelling is particularly valuable because it highlights the way that power works in Australia.

While the occasional stranded white explorer turned to Aboriginal people for survival, white Australia has generally been loath to learn much at all from Aboriginal people. Despite the rhetoric of self-determination, white experts still develop policy and programs for Aboriginal people, often without effective consultation, and then take them into communities, often to see them fail. A community development model, where outsiders work to help the community build a program for itself, is almost unheard of in the delivery of services in Aboriginal communities.

However, the aim of *Whitefella Jump Up* is not "to offer yet another solution to the Aborigine problem", but rather to offer Aboriginality as a solution to "whitefella spiritual desolation". But when Greer talks about Aboriginality, she leaves me bewildered. Where she speaks of Australia becoming an Aboriginal nation as a symbolic undertaking, the argument makes sense enough. This isn't a particularly new idea; the "pay the rent" campaigns of the 1980s were based on this idea, and the signs that have sprung up all over inner Melbourne reminding us that we are on Wurundjeri land are just the kind of thing Greer is calling for. It would be a good idea for Australians to keep thinking about new ways of describing, understanding and depicting ourselves, and to think about new national symbols that might be more inclusive of both cultures than those we have now.

Clearly she wants more than this: but what? Following the thread of the "adopting Aboriginality" argument leads us though some strange terrain. Can she be serious when she says that, "As a hunter-gatherer nation, Australia could play a further role in world affairs by making common cause with other hunter-gather peoples, all of whom are taking a terrible hammering." Does she think Australians both Aboriginal and non-Aboriginal should pull down our houses and head for the desert? Surely not, for later she says that in this new Australia British common law would be the preferred legal system.

Greer states clearly that non-Aboriginal people can become Aboriginal, because Aboriginality is not genetic; if Aboriginal people have to learn their own culture, non-Aboriginal people can learn it too. But there is very little in her essay about what taking on Aboriginality might mean.

After all, what is Aboriginality? Greer acknowledges that this concept wasn't even thought of before colonisation, when Aboriginal groups were distinct from each other and had no need to think of themselves collectively. In fact, in places like Arnhem Land, the concept of Aboriginality remains meaningless to those it identifies, with people identifying themselves with their tribe or language group, not with a collective "Aboriginal" group. But the collective concept is at the heart of Greer's essay, because the idea is that white Australians would be absorbed into this imagined community, and we will all be Aboriginal. White Australians are still learning that each Aboriginal group is distinct, with its own language; that there is no such thing as one Aboriginal group or one Aboriginal culture. Greer simultaneously exhorts non-Aboriginal people to learn about this diversity while amalgamating Aboriginal people into a collective identity at the heart of her argument.

As well as putting aside differences between Aboriginal groups, Greer sweeps away the differences between black and white Australian cultures, going into great detail about the crossover between them. This annihilation of difference is essential to her argument; but it is also an obstacle to genuine exchange and understanding.

I lived in Maningrida, an Aboriginal community in the Northern Territory, for just over a year, so I brought my experiences there to mind when Greer talked about Aboriginality. In Maningrida, we grappled every day with cultural differences. Living there taught me that two cultures could be more profoundly different than I had ever imagined. I saw that some of the problems facing Aboriginal communities, and some of the problems in relationships between black and white, were caused by deep differences in the two cultures. This makes solutions particularly hard to find, because they are likely to involve changing cultures, which is a disturbing prospect.

Health care is essential in places like Maningrida: the most devastating statistics that come out of Aboriginal communities are those that measure diabetes, infant mortality and heart disease at far greater rates than those found in the broader population, and life expectancy as lower. Health care, particularly preventative programs, involves teaching Aboriginal people to think about food and hygiene in a white way, instead of in an Aboriginal way. Aboriginal knowledge worked before colonisation, but it does not work in sedentary lifestyles, where people live in houses, eat introduced food and take introduced drugs. In Maningrida, it was difficult to think about the impact that health care would have on the local Aboriginal cultures, because its necessity outweighed the philosophical questions about the imposition of one culture onto another.

If we did pull down our houses, then white people would have a lot to learn from Aboriginal people about health care. But non-Aboriginal people won't abandon their culture; and the hunter-gatherer lifestyle Greer refers to is part of some Aboriginal cultures but no longer part of life for all Aboriginal people. The reality is much more complex, and we have to negotiate cultural interchange carefully. "Non-Aboriginal becoming Aboriginal" doesn't seem like much of an answer for white Australia; and it seems like a very bad deal indeed for Aboriginal people. What would it bring Aboriginal people, aside from an increased burden of educating white Australians about their cultures?

Our attempts to understand each other are often marked on the white side of the equation by a tendency to over-simplify. In debates about Aboriginal policy, we pit left against right, rather than working together to find some kind of truth. We continually romanticise Aboriginal cultures, at the same time failing to see our own culture clearly. In Maningrida, I met many white people who declared that Aboriginal people are "very spiritual", and that they have "so much culture". I would often ask them what they meant, and they would talk vaguely about ceremony and the connection to the land.

Of course, even if you could quantify "culture", you'd find equal amounts of it on both sides. But it's harder to see your own culture, and easy to see the exotic and unfamiliar. This romanticism often extended to the perception of all

Aboriginal people as inherently good, and most non-Aboriginal people as of less value. I came to think of this as "positive racism". It involves judging people by their race, just as the old-fashioned pejorative, excluding kind of racism does, but in reverse. Most importantly, positive racism forms its own obstacles to inter-cultural sharing and understanding.

Greer's central idea, that we can fix white Australian ills with Aboriginality, is a textbook case of positive racism, made all the more strange because she rails against the romanticisation of Aboriginal people, before doing it herself. Perhaps this explains the most disturbing aspect of *Whitefella Jump Up*. The primary evidence for – and symptom of – the spiritual desolation Greer describes in white Australia is alcohol abuse by white people, particularly men. In Maningrida, grog was allowed in under a strictly controlled system every two weeks – beer in cans only. And so every second Saturday the majority of Aboriginal people drank themselves to oblivion, and on these "wet weekends" the police and clinic were kept busy attending to domestic violence and neighbourhood fights. A suicide epidemic caused deaths on some of these Saturdays; and on some others, people were flown to Darwin Hospital with the injuries sustained in attacks and brawls. In between the wet Saturdays, a large proportion of the Aboriginal population of the town wiped itself out with marijuana.

These were the images that came to mind as Greer wrote that Aboriginality could fix spiritual poverty, characterised as problem drinking, in white Australia. Grog rips Aboriginal communities and families apart. It is one of the most tangible and most terrible of the colonial legacies, responsible in part for the destruction of some Aboriginal cultures. And so it seemed incongruous, extraordinary, offensive even, that Greer could mount an argument that used alcohol abuse as evidence of white spiritual poverty, and then offer Aboriginality as the solution.

Ultimately, in among the unconvincing pseudo-practical suggestions and the contradictions, I think that Greer is right in saying that our national life could be more informed by Aboriginality. Clearly a greater commitment by white people to learning about Aboriginal culture is needed for race relations in Australia to move forward. Many non-Aboriginal Australians have begun to do this in various ways, and we need more of this. Rather than romanticising Aboriginal people and their cultures, I hope non-Aboriginal people can look honestly at ourselves and our relationships with Aboriginal people, and try to go beyond the polarised, over-simplified political debates to a better level of engagement. And I hope that we will find better reasons for doing this than a quest for a black magic cure to white Australian problems.

Mary Ellen Jordan*'s book* Balanda, *about her experiences living and working in Maningrida, an Aboriginal community in the Northern Territory, is to be published by Allen & Unwin in 2005.*

GEOFF SHARP

The epigraph to Germaine Greer's *Whitefella Jump Up: The Shortest Way to Nationhood* notes that to "jump up" is to "leap up to a higher level … to be resurrected or reborn". Clearly transformations of this order reach beyond conventional politics. Just because they denote changes in the very frame of existence, they are also slow to define themselves within individual experience.

Greer is spot on in anticipating that her particular approach to "jumping up" would be ridiculed. Under the heading "The Great Dingbat Has Spoken" (*Sunday Age*, 14/9/03), Terry Lane homed in on Greer's notion of building on the slivers of Aboriginality learned from early contact with indigenous people and becoming a hunter-gatherer republic. In his enthusiasm to ridicule her proposals, he resorted to the type of disparaging rhetoric revived in the recent past by Tim Fischer: the genre of "they had no real houses, they didn't know about the wheel". Unlike the *Age* editorial writer, whose comment appeared a day or so later, Lane did not "sit down and think" long enough to entertain the view "that Aborigines may have something worthwhile to teach us" (*Age*, 16/9/03). In that same issue of the *Age*, Gerard Henderson poured on more ridicule. Under the "free speech" heading, "Germaine, Go Home and Shut Up", his special beef was with Greer's claim that the Australian landmass has been "crazily devastated by white-fellas".

I go along with Greer's general thesis that there is an increasingly urgent need for Australians to "jump up" and to begin to reconstruct the foundations of our whole way of living. Within the mainstream of Australian life that could well take in the recognition that the reciprocity which Greer tends to present as exclusively Aboriginal still retains a foothold in social life generally. Could it be that the problem for us relates to the recognition and renewal of what we already have rather than simply learning it from Aboriginal people?

The limits of reciprocity

That said, it is important to emphasise that Greer's essay has one outstanding virtue. It contributes to a wider understanding that reciprocity is nothing less than the social framework of a different mode of existence. It entails a different way of knowing and feeling both in the relation of people to one another and in their sense of unity with nature. Unless this is understood, "civilised" people and those who still live within a world of reciprocity will continue to talk – and to act – past one another. Greer suggests that Governor Phillip and Bennelong did just that. Neither of them could grasp the way the other differed. As Greer so persuasively records, the pastoralists then writ large that same failure. Exploitation brushed aside any prospect that reciprocal exchange could begin to enact a unity of some of the differences between the two ways of life.

My main theme is that in her often compelling critique of white Australian ways Greer has nevertheless overlooked the need for qualification. We white Australians do retain some elements of reciprocity. They persist in family life, in friendship and as an often taken-for-granted element of every social relationship. Certainly our reciprocity is different. It is affected by the institutions with which it is intertwined and by the universalising values and institutions which seek to mitigate or regulate payback. If, in the most general terms, we begin to define reciprocity as a give-and-take relation which maintains and recreates inter-relations between groups and persons on the basis of equality, that can at least serve as a reference point. It is inseparable from sympathy and empathy, and other traits which we typically assign to "human nature". I would argue that – within the limits of our species being – reciprocity creates rather than expresses human nature. To ignore that, to treat "human nature" as a given, is to be blind to its being undermined when its home base – reciprocity – is itself eroded.

Germaine Greer believes that white Australians have deeply suppressed their guilt and shame for having stolen the land. But I suggest that this is a quite secondary effect. So far as it does exist, it merges with a contemporary and far more comprehensive movement for ethical renewal and practical transformation.

Within that movement there is a retrospective understanding that we *should* feel guilt. Denoting a profound cultural break, that movement takes in ecological awareness, the green movement, certain forms of feminism and that whole shift of sensibility which, being only half-articulate, has yet to recognise its own social roots. As a basic social form, reciprocity lies within those social encounters which are quite direct and typically take place in the flesh. Hence they are in marked contrast to the external social connections and practices which have so radically undercut the core reciprocal institution, the family. Of course I hold no brief for the current version of the family or the distortions that may include. I am speaking more generally of a form of life.

Just because reflection about what we typically take to

be given is rare and difficult, any probing of these areas tends to be gradual and tentative. The gap between thought and action is hard to cross. Hence, through a whole historical period any movement for ethical renewal and cultural reconstruction of reciprocal origins is likely to be fragmented and given to expressions which sometimes border on the bizarre.

The *Age* editorial to which I have already referred went some way towards pointing out why the core of truth in some of Greer's general propositions could not serve as an effective guide. After first quoting her to the effect that "Aboriginality is not simply a cluster of behaviours and characteristics that individuals could claim for themselves and recognise in themselves; it is more importantly a characteristic of the continent itself," the editorial noted that, "The vagueness and romanticism of her suggestion is a real problem."

Yes, a real problem with widely dispersed roots. Greer's key empirical claims, whether about white Australians drowning their guilt in alcohol or hating the land, are unverified to an embarrassing degree. Her ways of supporting them are so tied to selective evidence that the opposite can be argued with similar force. Beyond that there are quite far-reaching problems of method as well.

Behind her preoccupation with guilt, with alcoholism, with individuals learning to be different, with jumping up as conversion, and for that matter with the psychoanalytical mechanisms – denial, repression, projection etc. – there is a persistent preoccupation with individuals. The collectively constructed cultural frameworks which define and delimit what we learn and what as individuals we can change never receive proper recognition. In matters of method she is an idealist, sub-species romantic. Her one-sided preoccupation with guilt and redemption closes off any real insight into the sources within white Australian life of the renewed appeal of reciprocity, of direct engagement with nature or concern for the future of indigenous peoples.

Drowning our guilt in drink

Before returning to these general issues, a pause to consider Greer's evidence is in order. In the first dozen or so pages of her essay, she elaborates the proposition that in the years following the arrival of the First Fleet in 1788 the first new Australians saturated themselves in alcohol. Her strongest claim to hard evidence is that, "Between 1800 and 1802 when D'Arcy Wentworth and his mates held an exclusive licence for the importation of liquor, 69,980 gallons of spirits and 33,246 gallons of wine were landed in Sydney, to be consumed by a population of less than 6000." It certainly sounds like enough to fuel a mighty hiccup. Assuming that only a dozen or so years after 1788, the 6000 (or so) potential drinkers were adults, that works out, by present standards, at approximately one 700 ml bottle of the hard stuff every ten days plus a bottle of wine every three weeks. Even given that the liquor imported in the wake of white settlement was quite probably double strength, 700 ml of hard liquor every four or five days still doesn't seem enough to cover up guilt and shame or to serve as an effective anodyne to the "shock, disorientation and misery" associated with settlement in a strange land.

According to Greer, early alcoholism carried over into the pastoral industry: "Ruinous drinking habits did not change as the colony grew; wherever the settlers went alcohol followed, and workers in every branch of the pastoral industry if they got their hands on alcohol would drink it to the last drop, unless it killed them first." Even today, "In prissy white-collar twenty-first-century Australia, a culture of macho hard-drinking still prevails."

Data on alcohol consumption circulated by the Department of Secondary Industry seem to confirm that Greer's thesis on the central role of alcoholism within an Australian culture of denial is distinctly exaggerated. In the 1970s the average consumption of *pure* alcohol for those over 18 years of age was close to one quarter of a litre (250 ml) per week and roughly equivalent to one bottle of Johnnie Walker (at about 33 per cent pure) per week and not all that much below the level of consumption that Greer suggests kept the first white arrivals more or less permanently plastered. When Australia is compared with other settler nations with European roots, its current consumption of alcohol simply does not set it apart. The same pattern of consumption also appears in other nation-states.

The anecdotal evidence Greer presents is selectively garnered to support her general propositions concerning shame, guilt and hatred of the land. The evidence for hatred of the land is equally selective as that for consumption of alcohol. "I love a sunburnt country ..." and all that is brushed aside in favour of the literary allusions which might support the suppressions, denials, displacements and projections which Greer calls up as she seeks to support her suppressed guilt conjecture.

As I implied before entering this brief detour through the bars and shanties of an earlier Australia, the effect of Greer's focus on guilt and its denial is to draw attention away from a different approach which might more effectively support the renewal within our own way of life of the reciprocity and equality she recognises as so central among indigenous people.

Two ways of "jumping up"

Greer's evocative portrait of contemporary white Australians concentrates on the rapacity, the greed and the crass materialism to which the later trajectory of the Enlightenment has brought us. She wants us to redeem ourselves, partly by actually recognising rather than denying the traces of Aboriginality we took on board in early contact. But above all, as she emphasises in her section on "The Big Idea", she wants us to face the reality that it is "we" who have failed, through our incapacity to respond to the generosity of reciprocal gestures, and not those who have lived on this land "since time immemorial". Hence her solution: embrace reciprocity, become hunter-gatherers. I am proposing an alternative: extend and renew the reciprocal forms of social life as the practical response to the widening understanding that our "human nature" is under threat.

Given the shortcomings of the guilt/alcohol/denial conjecture, the question still remains why a diffuse social movement whose members share Germaine Greer's concerns find it difficult to articulate a comprehensive alternative. Within Greer's own terms one might suggest that when there is no way to accommodate the stirring of reciprocal sensibilities, a social/psychological displacement operates: people identify with the far more explicit manifestation of reciprocity in Aboriginal life and so transfer any affect to a more clearly defined object.

But in terms of this comment a markedly different interpretation is available. First, one may point to the masking of reciprocity by the common assumption that human nature may be taken as given. The second point is closely related. Westerners have relocated their self-definitions within institutions, whether of work, recreation, media or extended neighbourhood, which have marched out from beneath that far more embracing reciprocal umbrella characteristic of the Aboriginal mode of life.

This is of course to refer to the way in which the Enlightenment, or more generally the whole movement which we privilege under the name of civilisation, has pushed reciprocity into the shadows. As Westerners we have "jumped up", not merely as the epigraph to the *Quarterly Essay* might suggest, subjectively, but in and through a far more extended fabric of social life – the market, the media etc. Yet for all that, reciprocity persists. As a mode of interchange it is something of an historical constant. Through its imprint upon what we take to be our "human nature", it is a necessary condition of every social relationship, even those which reverse or divert its ethical impulse. As, for instance, in the dog-eat-dog interchanges which are at the heart of every market economy, or the detachment and formality typical of the bureaucracy.

And there is another far more important and profoundly paradoxical way in which, in Western culture, reciprocity has been obscured. It lies within the psychoanalytic version of individualism which is fundamental to Greer's thesis. While derived from the analysis of family life, this individualism screens out the relatively equalising motif of reciprocity in favour of the hierarchical forms inseparable from the Oedipal story. As method it cannot see what it excludes from the field of vision and so in Greer's case it blinds her to the persistence within her own culture of one main core of the humanity she seeks to redeem by way of the "shortest way to nationhood".

Because, for us, the part played by reciprocity in forming our basic values and ways of knowing is hidden within a taken-for-granted sense of human nature, there is no ready grasp of limits. We do not readily understand the probable consequences of cutting away the immediacy of tangible connections both to the natural world and to one another. Having been imprinted with our "human nature" within the relations of reciprocity we carry our basic sociality into every setting of life – the market, the media, the bureaucracy. It is a necessary condition of the existence of these settings even when, in gaining their distinctive character, they strip away the fullness of that sensory order sustained within our now quite restricted reciprocal forms of life.

Is it conceivable, then, that the range of post-tribal institutions within which we locate our sense of selfhood could stand alone? Could they break free from the reciprocal forms which co-exist within them and tend to generate their own distinctive ethical frame? Here I am assuming that they could not. Beyond that I am suggesting that widespread and active in contemporary life now is an elemental sensibility which resists any prospect of webs of information as the frame of a future way of being. While its articulate expressions are scattered and tend to focus on single issues, they do find some degree of coherent expression through the green and ecological movements. Their ideology is the main source of the issues which concern Greer, but there is a difference. In Greer's case the solutions, whether implied or explicit, are to be sought by return to Aboriginal practices. This, however, is only one step more unrealistic than the green advocacy of sustainability as a long-term policy.

This is by no means to brush aside material assaults upon the environment. Our countrymen, in Germaine Greer's words, "insist on continuing in their madness, knocking down its mountains, grinding up its trees, diverting its watercourses, building high rises on flood plains, creating an endless nightmare of suburbia ..." But to be mainly concerned with issues such as these is to miss the heart of the problem: blindly accommodating ourselves to the continuing erosion of reciprocity, a main source of our human nature.

In some intuitive way Greer may have sensed this, but to look for the expression of that intuition in indigenous culture is simply to cover up her failure to look again closer to home. If more people were to sit down and think about that, one conclusion open to them would be that the shortest way to a viable future both for white Australians and for indigenous people is to renew our ties both to one another and to the natural world. This would mean taking back from the "progress of the division of labour" some part of those activities which have moved out from under the umbrella of reciprocity.

If this is one key aspect of the shortest way towards a

viable future, that way is nevertheless likely to be long. For the present, the dog-eat-dog values which erode reciprocity are still to be challenged by the rising sensibilities which, if articulated, might allow us to jump up within a different order of social life.

Geoff Sharp *is general editor of Arena Publications and a senior associate of the Department of History and Philosophy of Science at the University of Melbourne.*

PATSY MILLETT

One must sympathise with Germaine Greer. Despite her solid grounding in academia and a reputation built on finely honed argument covering a wide range of subjects, she also serves another, lesser master. She is a seasoned television personality – indeed one might argue a child of the media known to the majority only via her appearances on the box – and she must be well aware of the exactions of its voracious maw. A scholarly dissertation on the theme of white Australians and the advantages of their accepting links with an inescapable Aboriginal heritage would not have raised much interest or propelled her through the available TV outlets – versatilely stern and forthright with Tony Jones on *Lateline,* mischievously flirtatious with Andrew Denton. The key to her long career as a hit-and-run artist upon our shores has been to ride in upon a white horse of indignation and/or outrage at some aspect of Australian failure – pronounce upon it loudly and prominently via the media – and depart. This time she has chosen a no less confronting line of attack in suggesting we are "guilty inheritors of a land that was innocently usurped by our ignorant, deluded, desperate forefathers". Her "big idea" is that the way out of our predicament is to admit we live in an Aboriginal country – go back to hunter-gatherer values and embrace our own Aboriginality. To support this whimsical proposition she cites many cases and examples of where our settlers failed and how as a result Australia as a nation is little more than a basket case. Taken at simplest level – which is all the popular media can cope with – Germaine Greer has blown in again, this time telling us we should all become Aborigines. That certainly grabbed her the five minutes of attention she required to bravely (and articulately) air her views and remind us what a feisty old rabble-rouser she is.

The problem for me as a reader of *Whitefella Jump Up* was that while there could be little disagreement with her mixed bag of data from historical records and her overview of where we are going wrong, the whole did not credibly arrive at her remedial premise. Notwithstanding her straight-faced claim to being very serious indeed, it was of course a stunt. At best one should take with goodwill her plea that we sit on the ground and think. Unfortunately for the main line of the polemic, there was nothing unique about the mistakes made in the course of Australia's settlement by Europeans except that it was in comparison with every other colonisation in world history less violent and less destructive of land and indigenous cultures. (And ongoing alcohol abuse and environmental madness is hardly exclusive to our nation.)

Dr Greer herself must know the weaknesses in her argument and the refutations that are likely to appear in the correspondence section of *QE*. To ensure the spotlight for the short stretch of her visit she has, however, managed to put her topic confidently and boldly enough to at least temporarily camouflage the inconsistencies. She probably also knows that by selecting as a target for contempt that tall poppy of Australian literature *Kings in Grass Castles* with an incorporated attack on the author, Dame Mary Durack, there might be certain family sensitivities – such as that of this daughter – aroused.

In the introduction to *Whitefella Jump Up*, Peter Craven states that Greer is not preoccupied with the debates between Reynolds and Windschuttle – or the who did or did not do what to the Aborigines. Since the main source of contention in these so-called debates is the matter of accurate reporting, it is probably as well Greer avoids dipping her toe in these waters. (On what evidence, for example, does she describe Bedford Downs as "infamous"? Or is she merely repeating some vague hearsay as if it were historical fact?)

In citing *Kings in Grass Castles* as a prime instance of not only the ignorance of the pioneers but also the wrong-headed nature of their "land-grabbing" enterprise, Greer has allowed herself interpretations – and misinterpretations – of the book and the motives of the author that do nothing to bolster her case. In challenging some cavalier assertions made in the chapter "Going Native", I do not intend that Greer should get away with a dismissive "Well, they would object, wouldn't they?" In writing the first of what she intended to be a trilogy, Mary Durack took the story from the point of view of the people involved. She avoided in *Kings* retrospective comment on the mores, motives and morals of the day. Although a certain amount of dramatic licence was introduced (it was never claimed to be an academic work) the book did not "purport" to be the history of the Durack family. Two decades of research went into the most accurate possible representation of a family chronicle. (What a mean little word "purport" is – implying that Mary Durack's version was unsoundly selective in its account.) In taking on such a broad sweep of history, involving many characters and their complicated threads of connection, the author could not afford to dwell on any particular aspect.

She was of course guilty of writing history in such a way

that it might appeal to the general public and of daring to hope that her labour of so many years might actually sell. She certainly did not envisage an acclaimed literary success that has from the time of its publication in 1959 never been out of print.

Mary Durack was not guilty – and here I take very strong exception indeed – of pretensions of grandeur. Greer observes that the Duracks were descended from landless and illiterate peasants. Since Mary Durack makes this quite clear herself (though Patrick Durack and his siblings had rudimentary schooling and could read, write and figure) there is little point in scornfully underlining this fact along with the statement that the author has interpreted "flattering references" to a more distinguished "knightly" background "as if … historical fact".

Professor Dermot Durack, a son of Patrick Durack resident in Ireland from 1922, spent many years before his death in 1956 researching the ancient books of Irish families, official and church records as far back as they went to follow the early threads of Durack history. A more careful reading will clearly show that while there is mention of clan warfare, there is no claim to "knightly" honour and members of that branch of the family fondly holding to the French "Du Rack" connection were disabused of this fallacious belief. It is hard to see how the subject of (faithfully recorded) Durack genealogy adds any weight to Greer's argument. The inaccurate rendering gives the impression of being for no better purpose than to take a malicious and personal swipe at Mary Durack – whose modesty and lack of vanity were legendary.

One must also query Greer's denunciation of Mary Durack for her tendency to "romanticise the savage". Reproving of Mary Durack's vision (quoted in a passage that still reads with moving lyricism) of Aboriginal society as timeless and changeless until the coming of the white man, Greer then herself strays down utopia lane with an image of black Australians empowered with some sort of eternal key to conservation, land management and peaceful co-existence through the offices of their freely available spiritual consultancy. (Greer in Alice Springs claims to have experienced "a new kind of consciousness in which self was subordinate to *awelye*, the interrelationship of everything, skin, earth, language". Talk about DIY spirituality!)

Further critical and accusatory comments centre on Mary Durack's having written the wrong book altogether. Why, asks Greer in alluding to the close bond between Patrick Durack and the Aboriginal Pumpkin, was *Kings in Grass Castles* not the story of a lifelong friendship between a black man and a white man? (Why, one could ask, did Greer when writing *The Obstacle Race* not concentrate on those women in history – from Toulouse-Lautrec's mother to Pollock's wife – without whose admirable support the work of famous artists might otherwise have been lost to us?) The bond between two men who otherwise shared nothing in common is surely told with an economy of words that could scarcely be more affecting or explicit. Mary Durack has also sensitively depicted a mutual dependency which became the core of the ongoing black and white relations within the Durack pastoral company. To state that she saw the white man as indomitably superior supposes of the writer an insulting intellectual simplicity and a perception evident nowhere throughout her long writing career. Rather than expound upon this, may I suggest Greer read Durack's 1974 *Lament for a Drowned Country.*

To declare that "the ultimate purpose of a book like *Kings in Grass Castles* [name another "like"] is to elevate the squattocracy" is arrant nonsense. One would be hard put for a start to include the Duracks, but for a brief period of prosperity, as "squattocracy" with its implied wealth and power. Their initial leaseholdings in West Queensland and later in the far north of WA certainly covered a vast area, but the era of tables decked with "damask and silver" scarce survived a single sitting. From the time of the 1889 financial crash the firm of Connor Doherty and Durack (CD&D) became a saga of unremitting toil in a largely profitless concern that from the 1920s fell into ever-mounting debt. To whatever extent Greer would point to this state of affairs as a result of their cited ignorance of the land and lack of proper regard for the wisdom of the Aborigines of the area, the fact is that the Duracks operated from primitive homesteads in singular discomfort. They paid for their incursion on virgin land with blood, sweat and tears. Mary Durack's intention was in fact to follow a pioneering family history – for better or worse – through three generations: the rags to riches and back to rags; the thrills and spills; the joys and heartbreaks; the interconnecting relationships both black and white …

The ultimate fate of CD&D is signalled in *Sons in the Saddle*, the sequel to *Kings*. This book is largely constructed from the daily journal of M.P. Durack and his detailed version of events. It is wrong to suppose that the family were – then and now – unaware or uncritical of the shortcomings of the one-hundred-year Durack pastoral tenure. The final volume (never completed) was intended as a more clear-eyed and personal view of the pioneering enterprise and its characters through Mary Durack's own involvement with the north and her long association with the Aboriginal people. She understood very well the conditions and failures of vision that thwarted and limited the chances of financial success. The often troubled element of black and white relations was only one facet of a tangled whole. (It should be said in their defence, however, that the Duracks were a great deal more acceptable to the Aborigines than what replaced them.) Such clarity of vision does not accord with Greer's censure.

To allege that the author might have held a careless disregard for the importance of Aboriginal people is not only fallacious but wickedly so. Tellingly, Greer makes no mention of *Sons in the Saddle* and no hint of *The Rock and the Sand* – the latter a serious and sensitive social study of the confrontation between black and white with the arrival of missionary pioneers in the north-west.

Mary Durack's life might have been more profitably occupied had she not given so many years to the painstaking documentation of the mythology and genealogy of Kimberley and Dampierland Aborigines. Countless hours were spent with notebook and tape recorder in Aboriginal communities, and the memories – including of the Durack years – of these people have been preserved largely by her single-handed effort and her unstinting assistance to those who later continued this work.

In 1972, when Germaine Greer was making headlines with her condemnation of "disgusting conditions" for Aborigines in Alice Springs, Mary Durack was at the Adelaide Festival. To her alarm, she found herself confronted by the press – (unlike Greer, she never came to terms with thrusting microphones and pugilistic headlines) angling for a Lady of Letters versus Fuming Feminist "sound-bite". Anxious to present a more moderate viewpoint, Durack endeavoured to explain to her ADD inquisitors that the influx of Aborigines to northern towns was a downside of equal wage legislation and their consequential removal from their "born country" by station managers. Not that equal wages or in fact drinking rights could (as she further attempted to elucidate) in conscience be any longer withheld. Germaine Greer was right to note the depressing situation in Alice Springs, but – she continued – this was only one aspect of a brighter and more optimistic future for the preservation of Aboriginal culture and art forms through the Aboriginal Theatre Foundation convened in 1969 – to which organisation she had given much time as an Executive Member. But by now the press had got bored and melted away.

When Germaine Greer was giving us the benefit of her

international perspective by being appalled, Mary Durack was one of the very few white people in Australia who could sit down on an equal level of affection and respect with a group of Aboriginal people and know their names, their history and genealogy. She did not speak of being "adopted by Aborigines" or such trite vanities. Seven years were given to the ATF (later the Aboriginal Cultural Foundation) on an entirely voluntary basis. The most consistent motif of her life's work involved Aboriginal themes – her deep feelings towards their situation past and present expressed in books, short stories, articles, talks and verse. To take her own chapter heading – "Who Does She Think She Is?" – who indeed does Germaine Greer think she is to presume to question Mary Durack's regard for Aboriginal people?

Putting aside more personal grievances, it is difficult to take seriously an academic who remonstrates against the first settlers' "mistakes" when such were listed in the lexicon of the day as enterprise, initiative, endurance, raw courage and, against all odds, a will to survive. Past damage can only be measured by taking into account universal white attitudes of the day – the awful God-fearing beliefs that so righteously colonised the world's far-flung reaches.

After a lifetime of close association and study, Mary Durack came to the conclusion that Australian Aborigines defied generalisations. Greer's essay relies upon them and in this failing alone "the shortest way to nationhood" falls apart. While Whitefella does need to Jump Up before we irrevocably lose our way as a nation, Greer's shallow handling of immensely complicated and multilayered subject matter just loses the plot.

Patsy Millett *is the daughter of Dame Mary Durack and her literary executor. She is currently working on aspects of family biography including the completion of the third volume in the Durack history begun with* Kings in Grass Castles.

THE LAST WORD

Germaine Greer

Too many of the people who rushed into print about my essay, *Whitefella Jump Up*, make the mistake of belittling their subject, so that one must conclude that they had nothing better to do. Some of the authors egregiously confess to being so hampered by prejudice that they couldn't address the substance of my proposition for fear that it was a "stunt". Only in Australia is my life of unremitting hard work assumed to be driven by an infantile need for attention; this libel is asserted so often that it is axiomatic and will probably feature in my obituary in the Murdoch press. I spend four months a year in Australia seeking so little attention that nobody knows I'm there, yet the sneering axiom remains unchallenged. Only in Australia is Greer "famous for being outrageous". Australian newspapers never commission me to write on any subject whatsoever, but pick and choose from what they consider the most sensational articles commissioned from me by British editors and run them under headlines that have been known to side-track a busy prime minister into condemning me for an argument I never made. This is the truth behind P. A. Durack Clancy's fantasy of my "ten out of ten for media coverage". When commonsense dictated she should have listened.

Clancy's way of defending the reputation of her Durack ancestors displays as well as I could wish just what history looks like seen from the whitefella's end of the telescope. A "well-organised, well-disciplined reconnaissance" can also be described as a "land-hungry posse"; it's all a matter of point of view. Clancy will never understand that Australia was in no need of opening up, that opening up was in fact evisceration, that what drove the operation was greed, or that the final outcome was disaster, any more than she can understand that my essay is not about her aunt who I'm sure was a wonderful person. Clancy calls me "a self-exiled academic", which will puzzle English readers who don't know that in Australia the word "academic" is an insult. Her determination to use the word is the more piquant bec ause, though I still teach, it's more than thirty years since I earned my living in universities. Clancy is not the only writer to dismiss me as an expatriate; Australians have still to understand that one could be a Martian and still write truth about Australia. It is a curious fact that they will accept the snap judgment of a reporter who spends two days in the country (provided it is a rave) before they will agree to consider the hard-won conclusions of someone who has spent more than half a lifetime there.

Clancy's cousin Patsy Millett, who is also involved in the Durack hagiography industry, is as convinced as she is that I wrote *Whitefella Jump Up* because I was desperate for media exposure. The sole ground for this belief is the fact that I made two appearances on Australian television in fulfillment of my obligations to the publisher of *Whitefella Jump Up*. Millett was not to know that I had repeatedly refused to perform (for a fee) for the insignificant Denton, whose impertinences I find unbearable, and only agreed to the exposure (for no fee) for *Whitefella Jump Up*, which, in keeping with his unassailable mediocrity, Denton had not bothered to read and did not discuss at all. Millett somehow managed to describe my demeanour with Denton (who was so struck by my indignation that he wrote an apology) as "mischievously flirtatious". Avid for any kind of exposure though I am said to be, I consent to my publishers' pressure to allow interviews about my work only for radio and television. So far radio and television have allowed me to give a reasonably fair representation of myself and my views, as interviews in print do not, but not to a viewer as astigmatic as Millett. She mistakes the tone of *Whitefella Jump Up*, attributing scorn where there was none, and seeing a analysis of settler mythology as a personal "denunciation" of her mother, Dame Mary Durack. Millett also states that I made "headlines" in 1972 with a condemnation of "disgusting conditions" for Aborigines in Alice Springs. I don't think of Aborigines as being kept in "conditions" like animals in a zoo, or of the Todd River camp as "disgusting" then or now. If I made any such headlines it's news to me and, as is usually the case in Australia, the words in inverted commas aren't mine. Clancy and Millett need have no fear; *Kings in Grass Castles* is still displayed in every airport bookshop in Australia and nothing I say is likely to reduce the numbers of people who just want a reasonably priced adventure story that insidiously and relentlessly displays white supremacy. The royalties will keep rolling in.

A more sophisticated version of the *argumentum ad hominem* holds that everything one writes must be about oneself, the view taken by the West Australian poet Fay Zwicky, whose poetry does seem to be all about herself, which is why I don't find it particularly interesting. So much more does Zwicky know about myself than I, I can't actually understand what she is saying. "As daughter of the priestly utterance with a vision of the ideal, her posture of defender of the dispossessed is theatrically compelling if impracticable." Cripes. I learn from her quotations of herself that Zwicky has been writing about me since 1989 and always apparently in the same patronising terms. Funnily enough for a poet, she interprets "the shortest way" as a short cut, and then intones that there are "no short cuts to anything worthwhile". You'd think, wouldn't you, that a poet would twig that the shortest way could still be very long. She should have recognised the echo of Kathy Freeman; after her win in the Sydney Olympics, with the media of the world pushing microphones and cameras into her face, Kathy said in an exhausted voice and her face stiff with a pain that was not muscular, "I just want to sit on the ground", turned away and did just that. When I say that we should sit on the ground I mean what she meant.

Les Murray is a poet of another order. I can't think why he agreed to comment on *Whitefella Jump Up*, except perhaps that he had a Germaine Greer story to tell. It is true that rather more than "a few" years ago Murray read his poems at Cambridge University and I was there. I wasn't "a lady" and I wasn't "in the back row" and I didn't assert. In fact I was rather hesitant about my question. I confessed that I had been struck by the way he read, by the liquidity of his consonants and the Aboriginality of his way of speaking, and I wondered if he would agree. He didn't reply "I've got any number of Aboriginal relatives". It wasn't such a fashionable answer in those days. He was a bit bemused by my question, as was I. There was no intention to trap him, but we have got used to Murray's irrational suspicions and I shan't take it personally. His idea that I want to transfer "nominal ownership of our country from Queen Elizabeth to the Aboriginal people" is entirely his own. The queen is not the crown; the crown is the landlord not the "owner" and the people would be us and we would have accepted our Aboriginality and we would simply claim the land for its people. Tired of me and my jejune ideas, Murray soon reverts to his own pet notion of convergence, not to be confused with assimilation, and provides a poem in support of it. We may be in the same ball park, after all, but Murray wants to own the ball.

As the latest of many white interpreters of Aboriginal society to the whites, having lived in Maningrida for a year and now writing a book about her experiences, Mary Ellen Jordan might be considered to have a better claim than most to take me to task, but not by referring to notions I do not peddle, such as "a mystical plane of higher Aboriginality". The clichés are not mine but Jordan's; because she thinks in clichés she cannot hear that I'm saying something different. Nor can she notice what I'm taking care not to say, the words I refuse to use. She and I will always differ about the success or failure of colonisation, because she interprets the devastation she witnessed in Maningrida as evidence of colonisation, and I interpret it as evidence of its failure. America was successfully colonised; settlers spread across the country and stayed there, so that you have urban nuclei across the landmass; you have desert conurbations like Reno and Las Vegas and Los Angeles, next to which Alice Springs is a truck stop. American hunter-gatherers have enjoyed head rights, a guaranteed income without hand-outs, since the 1920s (which hasn't done them much good because, like the Australian hunter-gathers, they are still in mourning for the lost land). Compared to the United States, Australia never got going.

Unable to imagine this different perspective, Jordan decides that my account is "inaccurate" when my position is actually opposite to hers. Jordan frets about what my proposed "Aboriginality" might consist in, but she would have been even more fretful if I had prescribed some pseudo-

Aboriginal lifestyle. Aboriginal people themselves could not describe Aboriginality, because it would be as new to them as to us. She vaguely twigs that the word would come before the fact, as a commitment, and then dismisses the idea as not new. Then she fakes obtuseness. In whose scenario would admitting that the continent is Aboriginal and adopting hunter-gatherer values involve pulling down your house and heading for the desert? It's much easier to hunt and gather by the beach, where most Australians live already. Can Jordan be the only Australian not to notice that more and more Australians are building houses in which living is done more outside than in and that our semi-naked children are out there demonstrating for sustainable development and down with the multi-nationals? If Australian official culture was hunter-gatherer, Australia would be committed to conservation and maintenance of resources rather than massive exploitation in the interests of RTZ and their ilk. If Australia provided the international hunter-gatherer forum, we could help to defend other hunter-gatherer minorities, all of whom are under pressure and virtually voiceless. And no, we wouldn't have to wear ochre and possum-fur.

My essay was not written for Aboriginal people or about Aboriginal people, but you won't be astonished, dear reader, if I tell you that their reactions were of overwhelming importance to me. Just as I don't know of any part of Australia that is not Aboriginal, I don't know any Aboriginal person who doesn't know (in his head) and feel (in his heart) that the whole island continent belongs to the Aboriginal peoples. It is important to me that ordinary Aboriginal people, as distinct from those Aboriginal people in charge of interpreting Aboriginality to their white counterparts, think I'm on the right track. If the central thesis of *Whitefella Jump Up* is not conscientiously absurd, if the right thing might be do-able after all, it is all credit to the patience of the Aboriginal peoples and none whatever to the captious and capricious whitefella. Lillian Holt's response to my groping suggestion was typically generous; she understood my silences. She saw where I couldn't go, what I wouldn't say, out of respect for the reticence of the people who've taught me the little I know. There have been other responses like hers, some from people who don't write articles for print, some from senior anthropologists who, while stroking their grey beards at my temerity, sent me papers of their own on the moral and political systems of Australia's indigenous peoples. There is a space where the idea is alive, just, but there's no hint of it on the op-ed pages of the worst English-language newspapers on earth.

Of all the responses to my essay Marcia Langton's was of the greatest importance to me. Years ago, when she was a light-hearted and astonishingly inventive activist, Professor Langton and I used to know each other rather better than we do now. Then we were friends and I thought we always would be. Now I am startled by the vein of nastiness that runs through her response; why does she think I boast about being adopted by Kulin women? What's to boast? She is perfectly entitled to doubt the "depth of my engagement in these issues" which must perforce be less than hers, but not to accuse me of "essentialist ideas about identity" as shaped by "race". The whole essay is obviously or, as Australians would say blatantly, anti-essentialist. Professor Langton calls me "Dr Greer" though I am as much a professor as she is and she knows it, and laments that I didn't address the question of Australian racism. This I didn't do because it was not my subject, just as it was not my intention to add to the volume of polemic clustering about Keith Windschuttle's amateur historiography or deplore the appalling abuse of Aboriginal women. Of course the view of history in my essay is truncated; what else could it be? Though my subject was not the suffering of Aboriginal people or the terrible offences we whitefellas have committed against them, this consciousness suffuses the whole short work, otherwise I wouldn't have argued that the wanton destruction of the continent is an expression of the whitefellas' frantic guilt. More seriously, Professor Langton makes a fundamental error in dealing with my modest proposal, in assuming that what I propose as a necessary condition for achieving any kind of cultural coherence (aka nationhood) I am also proposing as sufficient. In case I didn't make myself unmistakeably clear (and the title of the essay could mislead), let me restate it. Australia will never achieve political maturity unless and until it recognises its ineradicable Aboriginality. Ultimately Professor Langton, despite her belief that an Aboriginal Australia is a ludicrous idea, consents to move into the imaginative space of the essay. Once upon a time in the centre, she would have been less uncomfortable there.

Langton expresses regret that in illustrating two hundred years of misfit between the settlers and the land I didn't discuss more recent Australian literature, which she takes to disprove my case. Among the examples she cites is Australian journalist Nicholas Rothwell's *Wings of the Kite-Hawk*, which grew out of a commission for a series of articles retracing the steps of Leichhardt, Sturt, Strehlow and Giles. Rothwell as much as Leichhardt uses "the landscape as the sounding-board for his heart". Like Leichhardt he seeks in the kite-hawk of his title the "dark reflection of his own character". As he dashes about "discovering" a country that was never lost, he enters fully into the sollipsistic world of the explorers for whom the country exists to be traversed, described, classified, and ultimately conquered. Why Langton would imagine that such a book illustrates a new relationship between whitefellas and the land I cannot imagine.

Tony Birch allowed himself to get off my case and take the idea out for a run. He has a right as an Aboriginal person to think that I romanticise settler violence, but actually it breaks my heart that people oppressed and driven from their own country ended up having to oppress and extirpate the people of another country, perpetuating the cycle of outrage in an endless proliferation of evil. It may be because I have followed the desperate struggles of my Australian forebears that I feel unable to demonise them, but he's right. I didn't. If that's romanticising their violence, I'm guilty as charged. Birch was interested and amused to wonder how my "country folk" would respond to my suggestion that they take a long hard look at themselves in the mirror and repeat, "I live in an Aboriginal country". Well, mate, I've done it. In my secret Australian life, in Queensland, echt Hanson country, I made that very suggestion to one of my work-force. "I don't consider there's any difference," he said. "I see myself as Aboriginal". I thought that was a bit steep myself, at the time, but he does work in rainforest rehabilitation, eats bush tucker in huge quantities, and treats the land with deep reverence, and I wish there were a few million more like him.

Geoff Sharp's response to *Whitefella Jump Up* is to translate my argument into his own moral terminology and to congratulate me for something I don't understand myself to have done. His attempt to argue that Australian use of alcohol is not dysfunctional is valiant, but it doesn't convince me and I doubt it would convince anyone else looking at the figures for deaths on the roads or domestic and other violence. Still, I am grateful to him because he has understood what the space is that I want Australians to jump up to, which is not mysticism (of which there is far too much already) but awareness.

It was not as if I expected readers of *Whitefella Jump Up* to bear me in triumph through the streets and cheer me to the echo. It would have been wonderful if numbers of clever people had seen some potential in my idea of Australia as an Aboriginal republic and amused themselves by seeing how far they could develop it. I cherished a faint hope that the chattering classes might kick the idea around for a week or two, long enough to see if its time might not have come, but they didn't and it hadn't. It will come though; mark my words. A hundred years from now, Australian children will be amazed to learn that Australia once considered itself a "British" country. They will understand what a hunter-gatherer republic might be, and how the interests of hunter-gatherer minorities have to be reflected in international policy because they are fundamental to any notion of sustainable development. It would make me swell in my grave with pride if Australia got to lead this international conscience-raising exercise but, as whitefellas apparently can't grasp the lesson that blackfellas never give up struggling to teach, we'll probably have to learn it from Canada and the Inuit.

I expected ridicule because, though I didn't expatiate on the vicious racism that disfigures much of Australian society, I am well aware of it. I'm used to being patronised by the stay-at-home intellectual establishment as well, but much of what was said and written was meaner-minded than would have been considered seemly in the wider world, and made me ashamed for the people who had written it. English readers will now have the opportunity to see the essay in the context of the responses that it elicited, and may come to understand why I choose to endure the manifold disadvantages and discomforts of life in England rather than return to my birthplace. And before Zwicky gets on my case again, can I just say that for me homelessness is not a disaster? For me diaspora is the true human environment and homeland a murderous delusion. I don't sing the Ha Tikva any more.

Not one of the responses to *Whitefella Jump Up* so much as gestured towards the most pressing motive for writing it, though it was plain to see. Whitefellas simply look away when I point to the devastation inflicted on the island continent in a mere two hundred years. The denial of the disaster continues; the devastation accelerates. Two weeks ago, the British invertebrate conservation charity Buglife, of which I am a vice-president, had to protest to the Australian government over its grant of permits for the importation of European bumble-bees to pollinate greenhouse crops. Just as Nicholas Rothwell couldn't see the terrible wounds on the face of the Pilbara or the exotic grasses changing the face of western Queensland, none of these commentators has understood my genuine desperation. Australia doesn't owe whitefellas (including me) a living. They should stop ripping its guts out for a pittance, and sit on the ground. Sit on the ground, damn you, and think, think about salination, desertification, dieback, deforestation, species extinction, erosion, suburbanisation, complacency, greed and stupidity. As if.

June 2004